P9-DNX-589

"Kay Coles James speaks with wit, charm, and authority. Her life and home are a testimony to the truth in this volume. I recommend it wholeheartedly."

ADRIAN ROGERS
SENIOR PASTOR, BELLEVUE BAPTIST CHURCH
MEMPHIS, TENNESSEE

"Kay's warm, humorous, and candid style captures your attention as she shares from her heart key insights on love and marriage. She draws not only upon the wisdom she has acquired as a wife and mother, but also upon the experiences of others. Women of all ages, married or single, will find this a refreshing and honest look at what it takes to make a successful marriage."

BEVERLY LaHAYE
CHAIRMAN AND FOUNDER, CONCERNED WOMEN FOR AMERICA

"This book is vintage Kay James—chock-full of practical wisdom. Kay writes with such refreshing authenticity because her theology is thoroughly biblical, her obedience to God wholehearted, her marriage solid, and her life experience abundant. Whatever season you are in, there is something here for you. I especially hope that young parents will read it and become very intentional in preparing their children for marriage."

SUSAN HUNT
AUTHOR OF *SPIRITUAL MOTHERING* AND
YOUR HOME, A PLACE OF GRACE

Kay Coles James

with John Littel

KEEPIN' IT REAL

What I Wish I'd Known

before I got

Married

Multnomah®Publishers *Sisters, Oregon*

WHAT I WISH I'D KNOWN BEFORE I GOT MARRIED
published by Multnomah Publishers, Inc.
© 2001 by Kay Coles James

International Standard Book Number: 1-57673-781-0

Cover design by the Office of Bill Chiaravelle
Cover photo by Photodisc

Scripture quotations are from:
The Holy Bible, New International Version
© 1973, 1984 by International Bible Society,
used by permission of Zondervan Publishing House

Multnomah is a trademark of Multnomah Publishers, Inc.,
and is registered in the U.S. Patent and Trademark Office.
The colophon is a trademark of Multnomah Publishers, Inc.

Printed in the United States of America

ALL RIGHTS RESERVED
No part of this publication may be reproduced, stored in a retrieval system, or
transmitted, in any form or by any means—electronic, mechanical, photo-
copying, recording, or otherwise—without prior written permission.
For information:

MULTNOMAH PUBLISHERS, INC.
POST OFFICE BOX 1720
SISTERS, OREGON 97759

Library of Congress Cataloging-in-Publication Data:
James, Kay Coles.
    What I wish I'd known before I got married / by Kay Coles James.
        p. cm. Includes bibliographical references. ISBN 1-57673-781-0 (pbk.)
    1. Marriage–Religious aspects–Christianity. 2. Wives–Religious life.
    3. Christian women–Religious life. 4. African American women–Religious
        life. 5. James, Kay Coles. I. Title.
    BV4528.15 .J35 2001   248.8'44–dc21   2001003321

02 03 04 05—10 9 8 7 6 5 4 3 2

This book is lovingly dedicated to my husband, Charles.
For the words and ways he keeps it real.
I am blessed to share the covenant of marriage
with a faithful friend and caring companion.

So she became his wife, and he loved her.

GENESIS 24:67

Contents

Acknowledgments

Many voices and many experiences contributed to this book. I am grateful to the women who attended the Renewing the Heart conference series hosted by Focus on the Family. Their questions, struggles, and stories encouraged me to write this book.

To my family and friends, especially Kristine Bramsen, Rita Coles, Paul Conway, Nancy Dean, Dawn Hively, David and Debra James, Dr. Timothy Kelly, Marianne Dean Littel, Ruth McGinn, Carol Simpson, Lori Martin, and Lisa White: I deeply appreciate the time spent editing, talking, and sharing. Know that your impact on this work was significant.

And to my own mentors, Beth York and Joyce Ranson: Thank you for the special roles you have played, and continue to play, in shaping my own marriage.

Introduction

When I got married, I knew at a certain level that it was for life. At the time, my somewhat limited understanding of commitment had been shaped more by my own experience of watching covenants unravel than by any deep theological understanding. As a result, I lacked the conviction that my husband, Charles, would not—could not—leave me under any circumstances and that my leaving him was not an option. I knew then how special marriage was, but I didn't quite comprehend the profound mystery involved, how sacred and blessed this covenant truly was. Nor did I know much about the mystery of everyday living in a relationship with another person.

Building a godly marriage, I soon learned, is a difficult and lifelong endeavor for both men and women. There are so many things I wish I had known as I was planning for the big day, and later in the first year of marriage, and in the next ten years.

Today the nuclear family is quite different from what it was forty, even twenty years ago. Career options, enhanced educational prospects, and better housing, among other things, have combined to offer women more opportunities and challenges. Husband and wife truly are equal partners in the responsibilities of raising a family. Some of the literature of the sixties and seventies only exacerbated these changes by creating a false conflict between biblical imperatives and practical realities. As a result, more and more women are seeking help in their marriages—from pastors, therapists, the Internet, and marriage books—than ever before.

The fact is that there are some things your mother cannot bring herself to discuss with you. Your sister, if you're fortunate enough to have one, is often just as confused as you are. So who is supposed to tell you the "real deal," the unadulterated truth? In the African American community, there is a term for just such a person: a *sister-girlfriend*. Doesn't that say it all? Part sister, part friend, she is someone who loves you dearly and will always be honest. She will never avoid the difficult subjects or shy away from speaking the truth in love. Wisdom and prudence come as easily to these women as do straight talk and sassy commentary. These are the women who, as they develop godly character and achieve the wisdom of age, go on to be the "mothers" of the church. (This is something unique to the black church community: a well-respected woman with worn knees, a well-used Bible, and candy in her purse for children, who has earned the privilege of saying exactly what she thinks. Incidentally, when people ask me what my own goal in life is, it quite simply is to become one of these women—hat and all!)

Women have learned much about gender differences and marriages. Yet despite all of these advances, straight talk and the sister-girlfriends who can offer it are sorely needed today. Some of us, for instance, naively believe that divorce could not happen to us. But the truth stands in stark contrast to what we believe. According to a 1999 study of the family by the Barna Group, the divorce rate among those who identified themselves as Christians was higher than among the general public.[1] How could this be, I wondered, if one truly studied Scripture? Marriage is clearly one of the most important covenants and one where vows are made for life. Yet this year more than 40 percent of marriages will end in divorce,[2] with consequences reaching far beyond the lives of the two adults involved.

I was always intrigued by the instructions for women found in the book of Titus. Paul stated that the older women were to "train the younger women to love their husbands and children, to be self-controlled and pure, to be busy at home, to be kind, and to be subject to their husbands so that no one will malign the word of God" (Titus 2:4–5). Paul did not encourage us to inspire younger women or even to teach or counsel them. Instead we are to train them how to be wives to their husbands. Most of the marriage books on the market today talk about communication, consideration, and compromise, all of which are critical elements of healthy marriages. I am not certain, though, that we are doing all we can, as individuals or as a society, to help "train" young people in an honest, straightforward manner as they prepare for lasting relationships. Hopefully, this book will bring some of the sage advice a sister-girlfriend could offer regarding real-life issues confronting young women as they begin their marriages.

If you have heard me speak, you know that I believe in telling it like it is. Whether it is because of my cultural and ethnic background or because I was raised by a mother who believed in shooting straight, I have never been one to beat around the bush. In fact, some Christian books on marriage and parenting did not appeal to me because they avoided the tough subjects and couched everything in soft language. In reality, as a spouse and as a parent you will find that no subject is off-limits; when you start defining areas you are hesitant to discuss, you are creating problems for your marriage and your children.

I am not suggesting that an upfront approach is not difficult, awkward, and sometimes downright embarrassing. But it's a habit worth starting. In our family, dinnertime served many functions: It was the best time to communicate "corporately" as a family, to touch base in everyone's busy lives, to heal the day's hurts, and to challenge and educate our children (not to mention showcasing my daily efforts at culinary creativity!). We wanted to make certain that we had the opportunity to explain ideas, concepts, and values directly to our children instead of allowing popular culture to do so. We told our children that at dinnertime they could bring up anything they heard at school or during the day and Charles or I would do our best to explain it properly. Nothing was off-limits, so we heard and explained to the children many concepts and words best left to your imagination.

One dinner, however, remains a part of our family folklore and demonstrates what happens when kids start to figure out their parents. A new friend from church had come to dinner one Thursday evening, and I had worked all afternoon to make certain that dinner would be special. I had made a new dish, cleaned the house, and set out our best china and crystal. What I hadn't planned for was "word time" that evening. About twenty minutes into dinner Robbie, our youngest, then seven, looked up and said, "Mom, what is masturbation?" Needless to say, there were a few speechless adults around the table that evening, and Robbie's comment has outlasted all other aspects of that dinner in our memories. Shortly thereafter, we discovered that our older children, Chuck and Bizzie, had been giving Robbie words and coaching him to ask questions in order to "liven up" our conversations.

If you find yourself cringing at this story, then you probably won't enjoy this book. I am not writing it to shock your sensibilities or to be vulgar or obscene; I'm trying to make the point that we need to be willing to talk about anything and everything. And we need to have these discussions with our daughters and friends *before* they say, "I do." Despite all of our advances in communication and education, far too many marriages will end in divorce this year, and far too many children will find themselves in broken homes. With the state of marriage in America today and with the hunger that exists among women for honesty, truth, and help, we need real, practical, straightforward advice and a willingness to speak honestly with one another.

Charles and I made a decision to be open and vulnerable with those we have counseled on marriage and family over the years. We recognized what a difference it would have made if people in our lives and those in leadership had done this for us. Being open is not always easy; it requires finding the correct balance of openness and honesty without embarrassing people or revealing inappropriate information. I am not talking about the seemingly happy and overly sappy relationships that some couples are so willing to share on Christian television or radio. What I mean is a willingness to come together as two flawed but loving individuals, understanding the struggle that lies ahead, committing to the lifelong covenant, and being honest and open about that process with others. And so, we share. It may help; it may not.

I was blessed to have a wonderful mother, who, despite very difficult circumstances, taught us the value of family and the virtues of unconditional love, acceptance, honesty, and sacrifice. Whenever I think I have to sacrifice or give something up because I am a parent, I think about the choices my mother had to make. In what must have been the most heart-wrenching decision of her life, she sent me and two of my brothers to be raised separately by aunts, knowing that the stability of a two-parent, middle-class family would be critical to our futures.

My view of marriage was also strongly influenced by several books. One of the individuals who had the most influence on me when I first began my own family was Edith Schaeffer, wife of the renowned theologian Francis Schaeffer and cofounder, with her husband, of the L'Abri movement. Even in the midst of all the toil and trouble, she writes, comes an astounding joy and absolute fulfillment that makes the family so special—to us and to the God who created us.

As our only daughter, Bizzie, prepared for her own marriage, I began to collect what I considered the most important ideas about premarriage and early marriage. Along the way, I began sharing these ideas in the speeches and meditations I gave to women's groups across the nation. The hunger and responses were overwhelming, so I have tried to squeeze all that I learned into this book.

This book has benefited from lots of input from others. Thousands of women who have experienced joy and happiness, pain and suffering, in their marital and family relationships have given me feedback. What started out as "Gee, what is it that I wish I had known when I got married?" quickly evolved into something much bigger. I had long talks with the women who had been my mentors prior to and throughout my marriage. I had many conversations with friends about their own experiences or things they had learned professionally. At women's conferences and retreats, participants shared their stories. Strangers on airplanes offered me advice and anecdotes, and friends of friends of friends began sending me e-mails on the subject. As a result, I have been able to incorporate a wealth of knowledge and experience into this book that would never have emerged simply from my own marriage experience.

This last point bears repeating. Though much of this book

evolved from my preparation for my own marriage and then for my daughter's marriage, not everything in this book is from my own marriage. Without the many women who opened themselves up to me, this book would be much shorter, and the breadth of reflections, both positive and negative, would be far narrower and less helpful. I am grateful to these women for sharing their strengths and vulnerabilities with me so that others might benefit.

This is a book for a very narrow audience. Though much of what I have written may apply to you, I did come at this from a Judeo-Christian perspective. There are certain presuppositions about love, commitment, children, and faith that, depending on your faith tradition, you might not understand, agree with, or find very helpful.

Very few of the issues I have addressed in this book can easily be classified simply as preengagement or postwedding. There is a great deal of overlap, and generally engaged couples and newly married couples should be discussing these issues. For instance, the issue of whether to work inside or outside the home when children arrive is not something you are going to face immediately. It is, however, an extremely important issue that should be considered during the engagement period. Notwithstanding that, I have divided the book into two sections: Part 1 deals with some of the prewedding specifics; part 2 addresses some of the broader principles couples will face, particularly after they are married. In some of the anecdotes, I have changed the names and some details to avoid embarrassing anyone.

I don't want to imply that these ideas are new or even original to me. If you pick up any serious marriage guide or talk to anyone who has been counseling couples, you will find that most identify many of the same issues—communication, finances, sex, and so on. What I know today is the result of a great deal of reading, counseling, and discussing with some of the greats in this field: Jim and Shirley Dobson, Gary and Norma Smalley, Frank and Bunny Wilson, Tony and Lois Evans, Edith and Francis Schaeffer, and many others. I'm standing on the shoulders of some remarkable research, wisdom, and experience—which is what we should all be doing.

I also don't want to suggest that I have a perfect marriage or a perfect family. In fact, we are quite far from perfect. We have had to deal with many of the difficult issues that impact families today. Sometimes I think that those of us who speak out on pro-family issues are particularly vulnerable. Being married and raising children is difficult, and I don't possess any formulas or easy answers. I do not even have ten steps to guarantee success. But I do have a great husband and our marriage is a work in progress. I have three wonderful children whom God gave me to keep me humble, because kids do that in ways big and small.

I truly hope that others, including Bizzie, can benefit from this information, but I must admit that my motives in writing this book are also selfish. It has served as a refresher course for me, and the process of writing it all down has enhanced my marriage. One of the things that I learned this year is that even though someone may have told you all of this before, it is helpful to hear it again. So whether you are preparing for the big day or facing your first crisis as a newlywed or looking for someone else who might have gone through what you are experiencing, it is my prayer that you will find the comfort and straight talk you need within these pages.

Kay Coles James

Part I

Before the Ceremony

One

Getting There

"It's a girl, Mrs. James!" …
"Who gives this woman to be married to this man?"

t was difficult to believe that twenty-three years had passed between the utterance of these two phrases. As I sat alone in the first pew of the majestic church building, I realized how preoccupied I had been just minutes ago with worries about threatening weather and catering glitches and a crying baby who might disrupt the service. Even the music and the grand entrance had been lost in my thoughts about the details of the next part of the day.

Fortunately, the recitation of the familiar first words of the wedding ceremony, spoken by our friend and pastor as he posed the question to my husband, Charles, jarred me from musing about unimportant details of an otherwise important day. And just as quickly, I was overwhelmed by emotional recollections of my little girl—good, warm memories, such as learning that my second child was a healthy girl; her baptism into the body of Christ; her first day of school; the familiar smells of peanut butter, yogurt, and Play-Doh; the Helping Hands Sunday school worksheet of chores that stayed on the refrigerator door for two years;

and her lifelong companion, Curious George (a stuffed animal who now sat quietly in a tuxedo next to me in the first row).

Tougher memories came, too, such as the time when she was four and we stood by her hospital bed and cried out in anguish at the straight line on her heart monitor, or the phone call on a rainy Friday night from an emergency-room attendant informing us about her car accident when she was sixteen. And now she stood there, a young, beautiful, and godly woman. Yes, a woman! Our baby was a woman—when and how did that happen? When Charles replied to the minister's question, "Her mother and I," I wondered whether we had indeed properly prepared her for the wonderful, mysterious, and difficult covenant of marriage.

In the past year, I had served as the dean and professor of government at a graduate school of public policy; I was also completing the last year as chairman of the National Gambling Impact Study Commission, a federal position to which I had been appointed by the speaker of the House of Representatives and the majority leader of the Senate; I was involved in a number of other organizations, including serving as a board member for Focus on the Family and two private health-care corporations. In the middle of Bizzie's engagement, I determined that I would leave Regent University to become a senior fellow at the Heritage Foundation. It was a busy and fulfilling time in my life—but nothing prepared me for the magnitude and importance of my most recent title: mother of the bride.

The day on which Bizzie—the name Elizabeth had been called since her older brother mauled her true name—got engaged was one of those days (actually two days) where all of my roles seem to collide at once. My woman's intuition had told me that this was coming. For several months, our daughter had been dating Brandon, a good, decent young man who was serving in the Navy. As his service came to an end, it was clear that they were serious, and Charles and I laid out some steps that they needed to complete if their relationship was to continue (more on these later). All of these steps had been completed, and I noticed Charles and Brandon huddling in hushed conversations throughout the weekend, trying to keep their intrigue away from Bizzie and me.

Brandon had asked his boss for time off, romantically planning to pop the question at the beach that was the location of their first date. To his frustration, he kept getting delayed, so it was not until 10 P.M. that they set off on their date. When they eventually arrived at the beach, they had walked only a few yards when the beach patrol chased them off because the beaches closed at dark. Determined that this special moment would take place at a beach, Brandon drove another thirty miles to a different beach, this time without a beach patrol to intervene.

After they left the house, Charles shared with me his conversations with Brandon and what he had been planning for the evening. I was giddy and anxiously wanted them to return to share in their excitement. By the time they returned, it was after 1 A.M.—well past our bedtime on all but such a special night. Despite their long night, Bizzie and Brandon possessed all the energy and exuberance you might expect, so we all sat up in our bedroom and talked for a few hours. Then, after less than an hour of sleep, I had to get up to catch a cross-country flight to chair a meeting of the National Gambling Impact Study Commission in San Francisco, though all I really wanted to do was to stay and hold my "baby's" hand and help her plan the big day.

We had made much progress in the previous sixteen months, but the Gambling Commission was gathering in San Francisco to consider the language of our report, and I was expecting a long and difficult two days that would be both mentally and physically draining. When I finally lugged my bags up to my room, I admit that I was thinking more about a room-service hamburger, a hot bath, and, hopefully, a good night's sleep more than any nuanced policy about gambling. As I slumped down on the bed, I was able to smile when I thought about Bizzie and the fact that I had been praying for this day for twenty-two years. This was all part of God's plan for her life. It was my fiftieth birthday, and Bizzie and Brandon had given me the best present they could.

And So It Began

Not long after that, I received the first of many calls from Bizzie, this one about possible wedding dates. Huddled in the back of the room on a cell phone, I'm sure the press and my fellow commissioners thought I was discussing something truly important or involved in some kind of intrigue. I must admit that these conversations made the next few days seem a little more bearable, though they still dragged on and on. When one of the staff launched into yet another lengthy explanation of the differences between one potential recommendation and another, I found myself thinking about bridesmaids' dresses and music for the wedding ceremony. In my role for the Gambling Commission, I had had to become an expert on the subject matter, oversee the process, manage the personalities and competing agendas involved, and push for consensus in the bright glare of public scrutiny; as mother of the bride, I was also mastering the distinction between Carolina blue and jasmine fabric. One minute I was answering questions from a *Time* magazine reporter about the disparate impact of lotteries on African Americans, and the next responding to a message from Bizzie wondering whether an April or May wedding would be better (May, of course).

In talking to and observing other women, I have found this to be typical of what we do as wives, mothers, and professionals: We juggle many priorities in as even, loving, and considerate a manner as possible. At the same time I was making certain the bills were paid, the house was clean, dinners were prepared, and family traditions were maintained. In my case, this meant a husband who was commuting one hundred miles to work; three children that I naively thought would have flown from the nest by now, each with issues needing my attention (or at least I thought they did); a full-time job at the university, in addition to this increasingly time-consuming federal commission; and dealing with the emotional and physical changes that accompany menopause. In other words, young ladies, lighten up on your moms—our lives are complicated, and we're doing the best we can!

In a number of ways, being mother of the bride came easier to me than I had expected. I quickly realized how similar it was to some of my jobs in the public arena. In politics, for instance, the elected official for whom you work—be it the president or a governor or a member of Congress—is the principal. While he or she hired you for your expertise, skills, or opinion, it is his or her agenda and goals you are there to implement. When I worked for Virginia Governor George Allen, for instance, I would testify frequently before the Virginia General Assembly. The members of the House or Senate would often ask me my opinion on a pending matter. I would respond with the governor's position on the bill or issue. "No, no," they would quickly say, "we want to know your opinion, not his, on this issue. Do you really agree with the governor on this?"

Obviously, they were looking for an opportunity to put a wedge between the governor and his secretary of health and human services by trying to draw distinctions between our viewpoints. No matter the reason, my answer was the same: I did not spend two years of my life campaigning to be governor of Virginia. George Allen did, and he asked me to work for him. I chose to do so, and that meant that I agreed with his position, or at least his right to set the positions for his administration. What these members failed to understand was that I worked only for individuals that I had the highest respect for and that shared my basic principles. If I were to have a disagreement about something that affects my core values—what I call the nonnegotiables—then I would have resigned, but I certainly would not have aired my reasons for doing so publicly.

Just as it was the politician who ran and got elected, it was Bizzie who accepted Brandon's offer, and it would be Bizzie who would stand at the altar in a year. This was not my wedding, this was their day. And although I would work as hard as I could on anything they wanted as long as it was not illegal, immoral, or a violation of a core value (my operating rules for politics as well), I was determined to make certain that the two of them made the final decisions in this process. (If your mother is being too controlling, let her know how you feel.)

The Norm: Topsy-Turvy

Many of you reading this book have already been through a wedding, and some of you will be preparing for one in the next few months. I think we all have had a taste of how involved and overwhelming the logistics of the event itself can be. Now, I consider our family to be relatively normal, unpretentious, and not easily intimidated by what society expects for certain events. However, within days of the engagement, our lives and our household were turned upside down. The dining room, following my political training, became the wedding "war room."

Books, charts, fabric samples, phone logs, and file boxes littered the space previously reserved for entertaining. I *had* to be organized—one small oversight could mean disaster. We had spreadsheets for the finances, detailed information forms for each guest, time lines for every segment of the day, and to-do lists for each member of the family.

My role involved the typical mother-of-the-bride responsibilities. I don't understand now how I did this while working a full-time job. With my workload, it meant a lot of late nights, very early mornings, and weekends spent looking at cakes and dresses and hotels.

I used to think that bridesmaids' dresses were some ugly thing that you wore once and then threw away. I did not realize that you had to spend hours finding the right style and then more hours choosing the right fabric. Then there were the wedding invitations. I thought you chose between cream and white and that was it. Now there are more than a hundred different types of stationery that you can use, not to mention colors, fonts, and ribbons.

I knew that I would need some expert help and asked a friend of ours to coordinate the wedding. I first came to know Marianne as an employee back in the Bush administration, and she and her husband have become an important part of our extended family. She was someone whom we had always admired for her taste and graciousness, and we knew she would be able to help us novices navigate the proper etiquette and protocol of a big, old-fashioned, formal wedding.

But Marianne (who is white) had never done a wedding for black people before. She kept getting hung up on the appropriate length of the dresses for that time of day and how we needed to have Crane's paper and interview local artists to do the calligraphy.

At one point I said, "Honey, this is a black wedding, and all that we care about is that the food better be good and the music better be right. Nobody, and I mean nobody, in our family is going to hold that invitation up to see if it's printed on Crane's paper. But if we run out of chicken wings or the music is terrible, we are in big trouble!" (By the way, the dresses were the appropriate length, the engraved stationery was Crane's, and a calligrapher addressed the invitations. We did have plenty of wings, and the music was great!)

The event became all-consuming: Every family conversation was about "the wedding"; we called on friends for their expertise and wisdom; we scoured the Internet and catalogs for suggestions. I had an unexplained desire to attend every wedding to which we were invited, regardless of where it was held or how well we knew the bride or groom. I studied flower arrangements at every banquet I attended. I listened with a newfound interest to classical music. I tried to discern the difference between what we "had" to have and what it would be "really neat" to have—all in collaboration with Bizzie and Brandon, of course.

The men in our family adapted quickly. For the first day or two, they were eager to share in the excitement of this new endeavor, offering their own suggestions and asking questions. Soon, however, they learned to avoid me or Bizzie, quickly departing rooms we entered as if we were carrying some disease. I knew that they would survive, though, when they started couching everything they wanted in terms of the wedding. "This tie would be really nice for the rehearsal dinner." "Cable-modem access would help us find wedding things on the Internet a lot faster." "Maybe I should go ahead and get a nicer car if I'm going to be driving guests around during the wedding."

Though they probably became sick of hearing about it at my

office, no one avoided the subject there. Whenever I brought up a project that was behind schedule or something that had not been completed, one of my employees quickly asked how the wedding was going. Inevitably, whatever it was that had sparked my interest was quickly replaced with tales of wedding planning nightmares and the scrutiny of my staff's work got a brief reprieve.

And the expense? Ouch. The simple excitement of the engagement quickly gave way to the reality of what is involved in a wedding today. Though we worked hard to give Bizzie a wonderful day, we were not, by any means, extravagant or wasteful. Nevertheless, when we added up each item, the cost far exceeded what Charles and I earned for the first few years of our own marriage. (Please remember: It's important that whatever your circumstances, the wedding should not break the bank!) We decided that we would pay cash for everything so that when the wedding was over, it would really be over.

To test our resolve each salesperson assured us that we just *had* to have this or that. One vendor typified the audacity of this cottage industry. I had purchased custom-made cakes from a woman in my neighborhood for more than a year. When she learned that my last order had been a groom's cake for a wedding, the cost went to one hundred and twenty dollars for the same German chocolate cake I had ordered several times in the past for forty dollars per cake. Weddings, you see, incur *per-person* charges. One of the benefits of a twelve-month engagement was the time to shop around, find discounts, take advantage of special sales, and earn extra income so that the wedding was affordable.

All of this prompted Charles, on several occasions, to offer to just give Bizzie and Brandon the money we were going to spend to start their life together.

Preparation or *Wise* Preparation?

With all the craziness and complication of this planning, we were fortunate to remember to correct our focus early in the process. The "event," however consuming and important it might seem, would last but a few hours. The marriage, by the grace of God, would last a lifetime. This had actually been the model we had all followed once Bizzie and Brandon's relationship became serious. In a statement that was only partly humorous, the oft-repeated message from Charles to Brandon had been, "No ring, no date, no touch." I am not certain where Charles heard it—perhaps listening to Dr. Laura on his commute back and forth to Richmond—but it communicated our perspective rather succinctly. When they did get engaged, Brandon came in one evening and said with a twinkle in his eye, "Mr. James, we got a ring and a date." Never one to be outdone, Charles quickly replied, "Oh, no! No ring, no date, *no ceremony,* no touch!"

Seriously, they both understood that there were certain steps that needed to be taken before they could get engaged. Following are a few components of what we believe are wise preparation for the lifetime commitment of marriage.

Preengagement counseling.

First, Bizzie and Brandon completed preengagement (not premarital) counseling. It seemed to us a little late to seek advice after the decision to get married had been made and announced. Usually when couples ask for premarital counseling, they are really saying, "We've already made up our minds. Can you just bless it so we can move on?" The time to ask a few tough questions of one another, do a little analysis of compatibility, and identify areas of agreement and disagreement is *before* promises are made, a ring is exchanged, and a date is set.

The best places to obtain this kind of counsel are with trusted persons or programs that share your values, not through generic "couples" weekends with no connection to the participants. So Bizzie and Brandon met with our pastor for counseling when it was clear that they were serious, but long before the actual engagement date. A year later, after they became engaged, they began counseling with our good friend and former pastor in Richmond, someone who had known Bizzie since she was four years old and who would go on to preside at her wedding.

Family familiarity.

In addition, Brandon needed to spend time in our home, with our family, and Bizzie needed to do the same with Brandon's family. Our family needed to get to know him, but more importantly, Bizzie and Brandon needed to begin to understand the personalities involved, the family culture, and the traditions and memories that help make up the person each planned to marry. At first you might think that you are marrying just him without realizing that marriage is the merging of two families and two sets of traditions. Many will argue that you are not marrying the family, but the reality is that you are effectively signing up, in a lifelong way, for the barbecues, weddings, and funerals of a whole new group of people. If Bizzie loved Brandon but disliked his parents, sister, or grandmother, they would likely have issues later. This might not necessarily be a deal-breaker, but it was something they both needed to know.

There are people outside Bizzie and Brandon's immediate families who have been important since the day each of them was born. Circumstances and distance may separate them, but I cannot imagine meeting these people for the first time at the wedding ceremony itself. Brandon needed to meet Bizzie's great-grandfather, for instance, so the ninety-four-year-old patriarch of the James family traveled to Chesapeake that Thanksgiving to give his blessing. Brandon had to pass muster with not one but five different Coles brothers. Bizzie had to go down to South Carolina to meet Brandon's family. They visited our home church and the many friends we had there.

In addition to their emotional ties, these individuals could offer their own wisdom and counsel about marriage to Bizzie and Brandon. Because of their relationship with us, they were also able to offer a perspective to Charles and me that was often very helpful. When Bizzie and Brandon visited some old friends in Northern Virginia once, the wife called me to tell me how special she thought Brandon was—not that Bizzie or I needed convincing. She told me that I must be very happy, asking what more could a mother want for her daughter than a decent man who loves her child. It really helped to keep my priorities in order.

Parental permission.

The last part of Brandon and Bizzie's preengagement preparation will certainly be controversial to some. Call it old-fashioned; call it sexist; disagree if you like. We felt strongly that before the subject of marriage was raised with our daughter, Brandon needed to ask the permission of her parents.

Let me explain. I am not suggesting that this is a hard-and-fast rule to which every family must adhere. Not every daughter needs or should even seek her family's approval. There are many dysfunctional families today, and, sadly, many of the elements of trust, love, and respect that should make up a family are sorely lacking. In our case, however, there is no one who loves Bizzie more than we do, no one who knows her better than we do, and no one who has her best interest at heart the way we do. We are blessed by the tremendous amount of trust we have developed with and in our daughter, and we know that she understands our ability to be objective and prudent in thinking about her life and trying to help her discern God's plan for her.

For the same reasons, I think that sons—at least, our sons—should seek their parents' blessing when they decide to marry. They, too, know of the love we have for them and our desire for them to be happy. Though it certainly may be viewed as a gesture of respect, they know that we will bring the same objectivity to their decision that we brought to Brandon's request.

When these steps were all taken, we knew that Bizzie and Brandon were serious about their commitment to each other.

A Spiritual Workout

Notwithstanding that preparation, this work could not end with the engagement. After the actual proposal, Charles took responsibility for spiritual preparation. Just as I set a time line for the completion of each element related to the wedding day, Charles laid out each step for Bizzie and Brandon to prepare themselves for the covenant they were about to make with each other. He worked out a plan for Bizzie and Brandon for their engagement period, which included premarital counseling with our former pastor, as well as a great deal of prayer, reading, reflection, and discussion. He taught them to pray with and for each other, he encouraged them to read both secular and religious works on marriage, and he helped them study the Bible as a couple.

You can easily do the same for your engagement period or find a church that has a similar program. I've included some appropriate books in the resource guide, but most of the books available in your local Christian bookstore on marriage and relationships are a good place to start.

I also became aware of a wonderful program for churches, developed by an interdenominational group of pastors in Richmond, Virginia. Entitled Marriage Builders of Richmond, the program was created in response to a visit by Mike McManus, the founder of Marriage Savers. The group's member churches have adopted a community marriage policy and utilize relationship inventories to prepare and enrich individuals for marriage and train older married couples to serve as mentors to newly married couples. This is a great ministry for churches, and I encourage you to check out their Web site for ideas at www.marriagebuildersalliance.org.

The Result

The benefit of being organized was that all of the necessary details fell into place. For me, something really hit home at the beginning of the wedding ceremony. Charles was standing at the altar, between Bizzie and Brandon. The minister had just asked the question, "Who gives this woman to be married to this man?" I could only stare at their backs and ponder what I had heard Charles say softly as he took Bizzie's hand and placed it in Brandon's: "Her mother and I have loved her for twenty-five years. Now she is yours."

Through my tears, the significance of this part of the ceremony struck me. Indeed, our preparation, our work, and our care were finished. Yes, I would "meddle" in their lives as much as Bizzie and Brandon would let me, but a huge portion of my role as mother and parent came to an end at that moment.

I wondered, had I done my job? In the twenty-three years between the life-altering moments of "It's a girl, Mrs. James!" and "Who gives this woman to be married to this man?" had I taken care to train her as Paul instructed in Titus? The answer would manifest itself in the life Bizzie and Brandon made together, but at that moment, I knew, with a deep satisfaction, that we had done our best.

As you face your own wedding and wonder if you are ready for the commitment you are making, you, too, can feel the fulfillment that carefully thought-out preparation can bring. Take the time; make the effort; you will reap the joy for the rest of your married life.

Two

Forming Families

We have all heard these remarkable words:

Dearly beloved, we have come together in the presence of God to witness and bless the joining together of this man and this woman in Holy Matrimony. The bond and covenant of marriage was established by God in creation, and our Lord Jesus Christ adorned this manner of life by His presence and first miracle at a wedding in Cana of Galilee. It signifies to us the mystery of the union between Christ and His church, and Holy Scripture commends it to be honored among all people.

The union of husband and wife in heart, body and mind is intended by God for their mutual joy; for the health and comfort given one another in prosperity and adversity; and when it is God's will, for the procreation of children and their nurture in the knowledge and love of the Lord. Therefore, marriage is not to be entered into unadvisably or lightly, but reverently, deliberately and in accordance with the purposes for which it was instituted by God.[1]

If you are reading this book, you are probably in one of two situations. Maybe you are about to get married and your mother or aunt or friend thought it would be a good idea for you to read it before you take the plunge. Or you may be facing the first (or second or third) crisis in your marriage, and you are looking for help. In either case, *hold on.* You are involved in what is arguably the most important endeavor of your life—forming and maintaining a family—and nothing that important ever comes easily.

Why Marriage?

As a bride- or fiancée-to-be, you may face some opposition to your decision to marry. In today's culture, it has become necessary to make a case for marriage and family. The first thing we need to do as women is recognize that the best and most fundamental family value is *to value family.* This ought to be obvious, but unfortunately it isn't! In fact, it truly amazes me how hard people have had to work to refute centuries of experience, biblical teaching, and common sense. The bond and covenant of marriage was established by God in creation. Marriage is the method ordained by God by which we create these units called families. Why? Because it is the best way to form character, to grow children, and to fulfill the deepest needs within us for intimacy and fellowship.

As Bizzie and Brandon moved closer to getting engaged, I was shocked by the number of people, old and young, who advised them against their intended decision. Young people today face negative pressure to not get married. The conventional wisdom is "You're young. You have a life ahead of you. Pursue some interests, live a little, and have some fun before settling down." It seems that starting a career is oftentimes more important than starting a family. Pursuing a hobby is more exciting than pursuing a mate. Building a bank account is more satisfying than building a life together.

So how do I make the case for forming families? I think you have to understand how big the prize is to believe that it is worth the effort. The union of husband and wife in heart, body, and mind is intended by God for their mutual joy. Marriage brings strength and intimacy that no career, however successful, can ever approach. Excitement, energy, and fulfillment in a committed, monogamous, long-term relationship are unrivaled by any hobby or human endeavor. In this union of two persons, comfort and security are stronger than any material possessions.

Marriage is also practical. You share the mortgage. Someone else is there to help take out the trash and walk the dog. You are able to say "I need a hug" and get one. You have someone who will compensate for your weaknesses and benefit from your strengths.

No one will share your laughter and the memories of good times the way your husband will. He is your companion for the journey, lifting you up and helping to bear any burden that comes your way. Marriage is a spiritual endeavor, uniting two persons in a holy bond.

And, of course, marriage is great for the sex!

The Statistics Are on My Side

Perhaps you are contending with someone who is too analytical to buy into any of the previous arguments for marriage. Some analysis of current data may help. It's plain to see that every statistical indicator reinforces the importance and benefits of marriage. Married men and women live longer. They have significantly higher incomes, savings, and retirement options. They are healthier and suffer less from depression, alcoholism, and substance abuse. And, of great surprise to many, married women are more satisfied sexually than unmarried women, and this statistic is even higher among Christians.[2]

A final argument, one that lately is getting more and more attention, involves the public good. I think that most of us can understand the importance of marriage in our own lives. We understand or crave the intimacy shared with a spouse. We can see the obvious and positive impact upon children. What we do not fully realize is the impact one marriage—our own—has upon society. Let me give you two examples: I call them the Petri Dish Theory and the Component Effect.

The Petri Dish Theory.

Though the family is often referred to as the building block of society, I wonder if a more appropriate analogy would be to think of the family as the petri dish of society. Just as a petri dish is the best place in a scientific laboratory to develop cultures and study cell formation, there is no better place than in the family to develop the interpersonal skills and character needed for life. If you cannot get along with your father, then you probably will not be able to get along with your boss or handle authority very well. If you are unable to have a healthy relationship with your brothers and sisters, then you will probably not be able to develop lasting friendships.

Most important, the relationship between husband and wife is second to none in developing character. "The first and fundamental structure for human ecology," wrote Pope John Paul II, "is the family, in which man receives his first ideas about truth and goodness and learns what it means to love and be loved, and thus, what it means to be a person."[3]

An example of this ecology and what happens when it breaks down comes from a Sunday school class I heard about. The teacher was talking about the ways we refer to God and the church, noting that one of the names we give God is "Father," which conveys all the paternal aspects of our relationship with the Creator. The notion of a "Father God" was met with blank stares and a lack of recognition. Unfortunately, because of the rampant amount of fatherlessness, these students were unable to grasp the significance of the term.

The Component Effect.

To illustrate the Component Effect, let me paraphrase a very powerful sermon I once heard Dr. Tony Evans, the founder of Urban Alternatives, give regarding families: Strong families are the building blocks of strong neighborhoods; strong neighborhoods build strong communities; and strong communities build strong nations.

Of course, strong families also build strong faith communities, and we know the transforming nature strong faith communities can have on society. Marriage is not only good for us as individuals; it is also the first step to a truly civil society. Encouraging healthy marriages and supportive families—what Lyndon Johnson called the "cornerstone of society"—is just good public policy.

So you see, your own marriage impacts much more than just your family. It is your contribution to the community and world at large.

What You Share

Shortly after Bizzie became engaged, she had dinner with us and some old family friends, Carol and Jack Arnold. Jack had been our pastor when Charles and I were first married. In the early days of our marriage, he and Carol had been there for us as friends, cheerleaders, constructive critics, and so much more.

Because they would not be able to attend the wedding due to a mission trip that would take them out of the country, we all got together for a visit, and, of course, the conversation drifted to the upcoming wedding.

It's always good to see them, and we knew that Bizzie would take their advice seriously. After some laughs and shared memories, Carol began talking about preparing for marriage, and I must admit that I was a little surprised at first by the question she posed to Bizzie. Carol told her that she needed to think through her values, goals, and faith, and then carefully consider what she and Brandon shared. Was what they had in common enough that if Bizzie ever had to go a day or a week or a year without feeling "love" for Brandon she could do it?

It did not hit me at the time how significant that question was for Bizzie and Brandon and for all couples considering marriage. There have been days, weeks, and yes, I confess, even months, when I did not have that warm glow. Okay, since this book is about keeping it real, I didn't even *like* my husband during some of those moments. If he were writing this book, he would probably tell you about *his* months in the desert. Those can be some frightening and lonely times in a marriage. What will sustain you, get you through, and help you to survive? Shared personal and family goals, core values, the commitment made in the marriage covenant, and a deep and abiding trust in God are all essential ingredients. Because Charles and I agree on so much, we can keep going, one day at a time, even as we actively work at maintaining and, sometimes, even rekindling the feelings of love.

To make Carol's point even clearer, think about the opposite situation for a moment: You both love one another passionately. The feelings are deep and the physical attraction is strong. But your faith is important to you, and he'll go to church only if you force him to go. He wants to have children now, and you want to let your career grow and think about children later. You are a saver and he is a spender. He is a liberal and you are a conservative. He wants a house in the suburbs and you want to live in a condominium downtown. If the flame dims for a while in this relationship, we can be fairly certain that your marriage will be in serious trouble and may break up.

I can imagine few ideas more difficult to grapple with for a young woman in love than this notion that her love might change or even disappear briefly. Yet, the reality is that marriage is probably the most dynamic and challenging of all human relationships. Just as surely as you will experience joy and intimacy that do not exist in any other relationship, so will you face difficult and frustrating times. Indeed, it is likely that the way you handle the tough times will have far more of an impact upon your future relationship than how you handle the good times.

A Decision Bigger than the Both of You

Marriage is not to be entered into unadvisably or lightly, but reverently, deliberately, and in accordance with the purposes for which it was instituted by God. When you consider marriage in these terms, you may wonder how two relatively immature individuals can make such an awesome commitment. Too often, we tend to focus everything on the wedding ceremony and little or nothing on the marriage. We see the beauty of the ceremony but miss the beauty and wonder of the covenant.

We sometimes also miss the fact that we are embarking on one of the most difficult journeys of our lives, one that does not begin on the wedding day. Long before that day, there is dating and the engagement. My theory about dating is this: When you are dating someone, the moment you come to the conclusion that there is no way you could or would ever commit to spend the rest of your life with that person, you should break off the relationship. I know that this is a hard thing to think about and an even harder thing to do—to be in a relationship and decide you have to get out of it. (But it is a lot easier to do this than it is to break off an engagement!) Conversely, the moment you know that this is the person with whom you want to spend the rest of your life, you should start the engagement process. Once you know this, the nature of the relationship changes. You view actions differently, the pressure to have sex increases, and your relationship with others is affected.

If you're considering getting engaged, write out the sentence *Staying married is hard work* fifty times. If you're already married, remind yourself that the hard times you may be experiencing are normal. Though I say this with some humor, I do think these points bear repeating: Don't underestimate the work involved, but don't panic either.

Because of all this, as a parent I believe that we have to encourage those who are considering marriage to do so prudently, and we have to be willing and prepared to help them when necessary. There is a reason that people say love is blind. It is. When you are in love, when you have that crazy feeling that defies logic and makes you see things differently, you are often not capable of being objective. Every woman thinking about marriage needs to be mature enough to seek as much wisdom and advice as possible—whether it comes from her mother, grandmother, friends from church, or just some sister-girlfriends.

For some women, the engagement period can be one of the most difficult periods of life. Despite the whirlwind of planning that is going on, it is during this period that you must carefully and prayerfully consider the step you are about to take. In the previous chapter, I discussed some of the steps Bizzie and Brandon took prior to and after getting engaged. Let me suggest four specific recommendations here for any engaged couple.

1. Evaluate.

Assess your decision in as objective a manner as possible. You must have the strength to be willing to end the engagement if you do not believe that marriage is the appropriate step. There is a reason that we do not go straight from the proposal to the wedding chapel. The engagement period is not just for planning the event; it is also for thinking through what it means to be married and, specifically, what it means to be married to this individual.

Now, sometimes you might have the strength to call off the marriage, but you are worried about the fallout with your family. Please don't be. This is one of the most important decisions in your life, and you cannot allow your worry about hurt feelings to cause you to make a terrible mistake. A few minutes or days of embarrassment and hurt feelings are far easier to handle than months or years of a troubled marriage.

Over and over, Charles and I explained to Bizzie and Brandon that we could and would stop the process at any time. In fact, the very last thing Charles asked Bizzie before they walked down the aisle at church was whether she was certain about it, reminding her that it was simple to stop what they were about to do. We even had a backup plan for calling off the wedding on the wedding day: I would call upon my best speech-making skills at the church and then invite everyone to the hotel for a really great party. Though we joked about this often, we really did want Bizzie and Brandon to know that if they felt any doubt, either one of them could call off the wedding at any time.

2. Get Counsel.

Seek the counsel and advice of others, especially older women. It is particularly important that you do this before you get married, and the first step, evaluation, is far easier when you have the wisdom of others to consider. Bizzie walked down the aisle on her wedding day far better prepared than I did. Much of this is owed to the wisdom of women like her grandmother, aunts, and my own mentors, as well as Bizzie's willingness to hear the advice of "friends of Kay"—Carol, Sue, Mariam, Ginni, Marianne, and many others.

3. Abstain.

Let me be blunt: You should not engage in sexual relations before marriage. I believe that all women should wait until marriage to have sex. Many women do not. But that does not mean that this situation cannot be changed or a mistake rectified. If you have been engaged in sexual relations with your boyfriend before getting engaged—whether just once or on a regular basis—*stop!* I'm told by many young women that there is a prevailing sense that if it isn't full intercourse, it isn't sex and, therefore, is acceptable before marriage. Let's be clear: Whatever it is—heavy petting, a "hookup," oral sex, or whatever you call it—it is sexual relations and it is inappropriate. I am reminded of the old black pastor who upon seeing a young woman wearing a very short skirt walk into church remarked, "I can see all the way up Hallelujah Boulevard." Save the strolls down Hallelujah Boulevard until after the wedding!

Abstaining from sex during your engagement, whether as part of a lifelong commitment or a return to this state, will do a number of things: It can begin to restore the special nature of marital sex, it will help you to think more clearly, and it will remind your fiancé of one of the important benefits of marriage.

Unfortunately, the reverse is often true. Once the ring is on the finger, the rationalizations begin: "We're married in the eyes of God, and we're committed to each other for life, so why wait?" Many young women who have abstained until they are engaged believe that being engaged is a license to go ahead. It is not. In spite of your rationalization, until the minister says, "I now pronounce you man and wife," you are not joined. Marriage requires discipline—including sexual discipline—and if you cannot be disciplined during the engagement, you will have some problems down the road.

4. Pray.

When you view the wedding covenant with the reverence and mystery it deserves, it is evident that it merits a great deal of prayer. Pray for guidance, understanding, and an openness to try to discern God's plan for your life. Hopefully this is not something new for you.

From the time I found out that I was pregnant with each of my children, I prayed three things for them. I prayed that each child would know and love God. I prayed that they would be accepted into the "right" colleges, knowing that this was important not only because of the education, but also because it would be the time when their philosophy and theology and many life-long friendships would crystallize. And I prayed that each would meet a spouse who loved God and who loved my child completely.

My prayer for Bizzie now is that she will know how important her marriage is—to herself, to Brandon, to her family, and to our culture. That she will know, as Edith Schaeffer wrote, that "families are worth fighting for, worth calling a career and worth the dignity of hard work."[4] And that she will rejoice in the blessings and good times and be strong and true in the difficult ones.

As you prepare for this vital and awesome endeavor—forming and maintaining a family—do so with careful evaluation, counsel, abstinence, and prayer. You, too, will rejoice, be strong, and be true throughout your new life.

Three

Understanding
Forever

In the name of God, I, Elizabeth Joyce, take you, Brandon Blaine, to be my husband, to have and to hold from this day forward; for better and for worse; for richer and for poorer; in sickness and in health; to love and to cherish, until we are parted by death. This is my solemn vow.

All the months of planning were finally over. While Charles and I settled in to assess the damage to our bank account, it was time for Bizzie and Brandon to start their own family and to begin to live the vows they had made to each other. If a single sentence could capture the amazing combination of joy, intimacy, love, and frustration that marriage represents better than this vow, I cannot imagine it. Even after twenty-eight years of marriage, for me the echo of these promises in each day of our lives together astounds me.

As is true for most newlyweds, Bizzie and Brandon's new life together is filled with all the joy and fresh expectation of young love. It is not spent contemplating these vows and their implications on their lives but thinking about where to put all of their new appliances, coordinating schedules, and learning about each other. For our part, though, her father and I have reenergized our prayer life because we know they are going to need it.

Perhaps the most significant thing that I wish I had known and understood earlier in my marriage was that forever meant *forever*. I know it sounds silly to even suggest such a thing, and when I brought it up with Bizzie before she got married, she looked at me as if I were crazy. It was about seven years into our marriage before I realized what the true meaning of *forever* was. I'm not sure that a lot of young people have been able to figure out this concept.

I think I knew intellectually what *forever* meant. I think I knew it even as we stood in the church before the pastor and took our vows. I knew I did not believe in divorce, but later, as the practical implications of *forever* started sinking in, the impact was overwhelming. I had not realized that no matter how mad I was at Charles, how much he was not "meeting my needs," how much we were not communicating, or how much he was getting on my last nerve, that *forever* actually meant…*forever*. Imagine my waking up one morning, angry as I could be (though I cannot remember why), and looking at this half-naked man in my bed, knowing that I could not get rid of him! I wanted to kick him in his rear end and throw him out the door, but I couldn't, and he wasn't going anywhere. Because forever really does mean forever.

Early in my marriage I was talking to a friend who was experiencing some difficult times in her three-year marriage to her childhood sweetheart. When she asked, "Do you believe in divorce?" I quickly replied, "Oh, no, of course not." But then it hit me! I wish I had accepted this earlier and realized that there is a period in some marriages when we stop believing the lies of the world, among them that divorce is a good option.

You watch your friends bailing out of their marriages. Then they come and tell you things like, "Girl, I wouldn't put up with that if I were you." Or you hear it at the office and elsewhere, people talking about how easy no-fault divorce is, and you are reminded that, despite the way culture seems to condone breaking up, forever does indeed mean forever.

This concept may seem restrictive, but in reality, the opposite is true. Once you close that door and take divorce off the table as an option, it becomes so much easier to think about the real options that are available in whatever crisis you are facing. Of course, there are exceptions, times when divorce is the only option, but to me those are very rare. We will discuss them in a later chapter.

Before Bizzie got engaged, Charles and I told her that as far as we could tell, Brandon loved her and loved the Lord, that he didn't seem mentally unbalanced, and that he was not going to lay a hand on her in frustration or anger. Short of any of that changing, we said, she would not be moving back with us. Because forever means forever.

Get over It

Let me tell you why I believe this point is so important. There is an important corollary principle here, one that goes along with *forever*. It is a tiny point that I wish I had known and figured out sooner because it makes a real and profound difference in a relationship. I wish I had known very early in my marriage that there are some things about Charles *that are never going to change*. Of course, marriage is about compromising and coming together, and each of you will indeed change to accommodate the other. But there will be many things about your man that will never change.

And I do not care how big or how small it might be, it will still be something that really annoys you! For example, Charles is never, ever going to turn that showerhead off so that when I step into the shower, the water doesn't come right down on my head. If you really want to get a black woman angry, mess with her hair! I have tried reasoning, threatening, begging, crying—you name it. He is never going to change! (I share that silly shower story because I don't want to use this book to embarrass my husband too much. Obviously, we have had more serious issues in our marriage and we'll discuss some of those in the proper context later in the book.)

It seems we all have experienced this in some way. You spend the first few months thinking, *Isn't it cute how he does that?* Then over the next few years you begin to think, *That's not so cute, it's actually rather annoying.* And then you think, *If I pray with him and for him, we can change that.* So you spend the next few years believing that God will make changes in his life—that if you pray hard enough and believe hard enough and speak it enough, you can make it happen and he will change.

Early in our marriage, when Charles and I would fight over something, I thought that if I just read enough books and high-lighted the relevant parts and left them by the bed...if I could find the right tape or article...he would see my point and change! It wasn't, and it still isn't, going to happen. And you know what? I was a little annoyed at God for a while when I realized that, for I knew that my God was bigger than any irksome habit or "irrec-oncilable difference" and was capable of moving mountains. He could change anything in this world, so why didn't He just change this man? I eventually came to the conclusion that God was using my husband for His purposes.

When Charles and I were first married, I was very insecure and needed a great deal of affirmation. Though he is very loving, Charles is not the type to readily hand out affirmation. I soon realized that I had the choice to be a wreck or, in the words of Bridget Jones, a character from a popular book and movie, to be a "woman of substance" and deal with it and move on. I would not be the woman I am today if Charles weren't the man he is—the perfect and not-so-perfect parts combined.

It is important to remember that you don't have to agree on everything. There will be a number of "irreconcilable" differences, no matter how in love or how compatible you are. Some are insignificant, but some will be serious differences. The point is to resolve what you can, accept what you cannot, and not try to win every argument. Most important, make certain that you don't hide from the differences or the conflict in your marriage. One marriage Web site, www.smartmarriage.com, has a number of useful tips and tools to address these points.

Aha! A Purpose

How freeing this thinking is! And it works, not only in relationships between husbands and wives, but also with parents, sisters, friends, and folks in the church. If there is anything that Charles James deserves more than anything else in the world, it is a wife who will look at him and see him as he is and accept him unconditionally. And I have a secret: That is exactly what his wife wants too. That is the real need inside all of us, so why is it that we can accept idiosyncrasies in relationships outside of marriage, but when it comes to our husbands, we are determined *not* to accept them?

This is not meant to imply that we accept behavior that is abusive or detrimental in any way (more about that later). Simply put, it means the ability to say, "I love you. I know everything there is to know about you—the good, the bad, and the ugly—and I still love you. I accept you just as you are."

Unfortunately, this attitude is the exception rather than the rule. America has the dubious honor of officially going from being the most marrying society in the world to the one with the most divorces and unwed mothers.[1] Just prior to World War II, there were little more than a quarter of a million divorces and annulments.[2] In 1998 alone, there were more than 1.1 million![3]

A lot has changed in the generation since Charles and I got married. Divorce does not quietly creep into marriages these days; it shouts a quick and easy escape to couples from every corner of society. Our culture condones the easy way out over the way of commitment, hard work, and struggle. It is not just a beckon from pop culture to do so; you will find friends, relatives, and even the church saying that this is an acceptable, and in many cases preferable, choice. And no-fault divorces mean you do not even have to come up with a valid justification. "So long as we both shall *love*" seems to have replaced "So long as we both shall *live*" as the solemn "vow" couples take today.

Separation and Divorce

Let me be perfectly clear: I don't believe in divorce in all but a very few exceptions, but I do believe strongly in the concept of separation. Separation was designed for a number of reasons: to allow spouses to cool off, to put some space between them, and to remind each of them what being alone might be like—but it should be a tool principally for reconciliation and the restoration of mutual respect. Unfortunately, our culture seems to skip over separation and make divorce an easy and "painless" option. The reality is that we need a whole lot more separations and a lot fewer divorces.

I am not talking about separation as an incremental step

toward divorce, as many no-fault divorce states require. I mean separation as an incremental step toward reconciliation (though it may not always be the case). Sometimes the best thing to do in certain situations is to put some space between spouses. From this vantage point, an aggrieved spouse can step back and look at the big picture, putting the cause of the separation into perspective, which takes into account the entire marriage. The offending spouse, on the other hand, can consider his or her actions and methods to reconcile with the other spouse.

I do not believe in divorce except in rare circumstances, but I think it would be naive to say that it can never happen to good Christian men and women. I've already noted the high number of divorces among Christians. While writing this book, I spoke to many women who really tried to make their marriages work, but despite their efforts ended up divorced. Many of their stories were heartbreaking, and some involved abuse, neglect, and their husbands' repeated adultery.

One friend told me that she believed marriage was forever when she got married. She did all the right things to prepare for marriage. She studied the Bible and marriage texts, she prayed, and she spent hours talking to her fiancé and learning about the things they shared in common. What she did not discern was his growing addiction to alcohol and drugs. It was only after they had been married for eighteen months and had just had a child that she started to suspect that something was wrong. When she discovered his addiction, she treated it as an illness. She got him into treatment, prayed for him, and learned everything she could about drug addiction. But despite her efforts, his abuse of alcohol and drugs continued, and it began to take a heavy toll on her and her son's lives.

This man was never physically abusive, but he would empty

their checking account and take the car and disappear for days. Sometimes she would hear that he was at a certain bar or a friend's house sleeping off a drug or alcohol binge, and she would go get him. The times when he came home high and shouted things at her and their son were the most frightening of all.

What do you tell a woman in this situation? She did everything she could to help him in order to save their marriage. She went to Alcoholics Anonymous and Narcotics Anonymous; she tried three separations, one for an entire year. Unfortunately, none of it made a difference. He left her bankrupt, frightened, and all alone, left to raise a young boy.

It was only after the devastating effect of his behavior on her son became evident that she was able to make the decision to change. She had done all she could.

Malachi wrote in the Old Testament that God hates divorce and grieves the suffering it causes (Malachi 2:16). My friend knows the suffering her marriage and divorce have caused her. It shapes every aspect of her life today.

Because she thought her marriage would be for forever, she was not prepared for life alone as a single mother. When I asked her what she would have done differently over the last fifteen years, she thought for a minute and gave this sage advice: "Kay, Christian women need to understand that according to God's principles, marriage *should* be for forever. But the practical reality is that sometimes bad things happen to good people." Some wives have no choice but to face life alone because of death or divorce.

This woman said that she wishes she had kept up her professional license so that it would be easier to find work. She wishes she had, as a young woman, learned to be more self-confident. It would have made her a more fulfilled person, a more interesting spouse, and a better prepared woman for anything life offered. She wishes she had been a more equal partner in handling the family's finances before things got so bad that bankruptcy was the only option.

And she says she wishes she had taken charge and intervened in her husband's life much sooner. Instead, she let her feelings of being weak, powerless, and insecure keep her silent for too long. After living in this situation for years, she finally decided she would rather be homeless than subject her son to a culture of abusing drugs on a daily basis.

Unfortunately, civil law almost dictates that she had to get divorced. Without the divorce, she was accorded no freedom from fear and remained financially responsible for her husband's behavior. She still says she was convinced that if he could be cured of his illness and begin to live responsibly, she would want their marriage to work.

Very few women will make such extreme efforts to save their marriages. The vast majority of divorces today do not occur because couples have exhausted opportunities for and methods of reconciliation. Divorce is all too often a cop-out, the path of least resistance. Reconciliation is hard, and many spouses choose to walk away from something so tough. That is why it is so critical for a woman who is planning to get married to spend time learning what a covenant means and being brutally honest about the character, integrity, strengths, and weaknesses of the man with whom she is about to pledge to spend the rest of her life.

Investing in Forever

One of the most common causes of break ups in marriages is change in one of the spouses. It seems to me that wedding vows were written to remind us of these possibilities on the wedding day: "For better and for worse; for richer and for poorer; in sickness and in health; to love and to cherish, until we are parted by death." We like to think about the happy part of these vows—better, richer, healthier times. But we might face the not-so-good times. Could your relationship endure worse, poorer, and sicker?

When I think about Ronald and Nancy Reagan, for instance, one of the great love stories of our time, I cannot help but think about how different married life must be for them now. In her recently released book *I Love You, Ronnie,* Nancy Reagan included a letter from her husband that epitomized the tender intimacy of marriage to me. "If I ache, it's because we are apart and yet that can't be because you are inside and a part of me, so we really aren't apart at all," Ronald wrote to his wife in 1963. "Yet, I ache but wouldn't be without the ache, because that would mean being without you and that I can't be because I love you."[4]

Today, as they both struggle with his Alzheimer's disease, he slips away from her a little bit at a time, possibly forgetting even her name at times. Their happy and devoted life is now just a memory for her, and every day it is a struggle to go on. Nonetheless, she is there by his side, sharing his life—for better and for worse. I think the Reagans understand what forever means.

Forever is a difficult concept, and it may take years for you to understand how it applies to your relationship. But there are some things you can begin doing now to learn to accept your husband "as is," which will be a sound investment in *forever.*

Admit it.

Acknowledge that there are differences between you, some of which might be important ones. Name them.

Face it.

Don't avoid conflict, particularly regarding areas of disagreement. A healthy relationship involves disagreeing in a respectful, loving manner (more on this in the communication chapter).

Confess it.

Be a big enough person to admit when you are wrong or do things that are unfair, immature, or spiteful. Don't be afraid of saying you're sorry.

Value it.

God forbid that something should happen to one of you, but it might. Honor the privilege of marriage and all it means in your daily life.

Laugh at it.

Keep your sense of humor! It makes *forever* a lot more bearable and fun.

Remember, *forever* is not a chain; it is a concept that enables us to truly enjoy the freedom of commitment. It is the cornerstone of marriage that gives meaning to the vows spoken in the wedding ceremony and whispered in everyday life together.

Four

The Choice for Children

We were making very good progress—too good. Just ten days had passed since Bizzie had gotten engaged, and we had already reserved the church, spoken to our minister, and made the initial arrangements for the flowers, cake, limousine, trumpeter, and string quartet.

Bizzie and I were sitting in the kitchen, talking about her conversations with Brandon, the wedding, and where they were going to live after the ceremony. "What about children?" I asked innocently.

"I can't have children for at least three years," she replied with the cool logic that only the voice of inexperience can muster.

My sense of satisfaction at our progress quickly evaporated. Here was a reminder of the important work that needed to be done before the wedding. "Bizzie," I started softly, "you *can* have children. It happens every day in marriages—women get pregnant on their wedding night, during the honeymoon, in the first few months. If you truly cannot have children in the first three years, then you should postpone getting married until then."

I did not mean to sound harsh then, nor do I now. But I believe this so strongly that I do not think you should get married if you are not ready to have children. Society selfishly tells us that marriage is about you (singular), but the reality is that it is about *you* (plural). You may have legitimate reasons for wanting to wait—health, age, some personal situation—but you cannot separate the reality of marriage from the possibility of children. As I said to Bizzie, a lot of people get pregnant on the honeymoon, or in the first month, so parenthood is something you should think about and for which you should be prepared. If it would be so horrible for you to have children at this point, perhaps you should wait to get married until you are ready.

There is nothing wrong with planning when to get pregnant. Bizzie, for example, wanted Brandon to finish school, and she wanted to get through her teacher's certification process. But it was important for them to realize that their plans are subject to God's will and the mystery of life. And, practically speaking, they needed to remember that every unwanted or untimely pregnancy does not mean an unwanted child. I reminded Bizzie that both she and her younger brother were the results of failed contraception and that I could not imagine my life without them.

Yet Another Important Decision

So, the next big decision to consider in your life as a couple will be whether to have children and, if so, when. This is a deeply personal decision and one that involves many factors, both real and perceived. Despite pressure from anxious mothers-in-law, much of our modern culture contends that this is a decision to postpone as long as possible, that children are detrimental to careers, finances, and comfort. These same arguments were also used to discourage marriage, and the same rebuttals apply here.

Why is the decision whether and when to have children so significant that it must be discussed by you and your fiancé before you are married? This may seem premature when you are busy planning a wedding or thinking about getting engaged, but it is critical that you know and understand your fiancé's feelings about this subject before you get married. If you have a difference of opinion, it is essential to work it out before the wedding. If you do not resolve it, it may become one of those issues that will gnaw at the edges of your relationship, and when you have some of those tough times that we all encounter, it might erupt into a crisis point in your relationship. It is far better to confront any disagreement before the wedding ceremony and, at least, come to understand the thinking involved.

You should also understand how children fit into the paradigm of marriage—not only the significance of the decision itself, but also the all-encompassing effect that children will have on you as an individual and as a couple. They will profoundly impact, in ways unimaginable, every aspect of your life. No one should ever be tricked into parenthood or surprised by it, though many are. It is something that should be a thought-out and discussed mutual decision.

Some couples embrace childlessness, calling it "childless by choice," a concept I find difficult to understand. I make myself vulnerable by even saying that. Intellectually, I know that just as some are called not to marry, some may be called not to have children. The reasons could be deep, complex, and even noble— involving emotional health, maturity, or vocational demands. I believe, however, that the decision not to have children should be the exception and not the rule.

Our culture seems to have identified greed, materialism, and self-indulgence as acceptable reasons not to have children. The cultural sentiment seems to be so overwhelming that I feel compelled to make the case for kids. Forgive me if I overstate the case, but I feel like I have to stroke harder to go against the tide.

The Case for Kids

How do you communicate the joy and importance of children to people who think they are just a choice? Let's set aside, for a moment, those dysfunctional individuals who, because of their own inner pain, have no ability to bond with their children. For most women, the act of childbirth will rank somewhere at the top of the list of life experiences. The pain of delivery is minimal and will be overshadowed by the joy. However, to keep it real, I feel I should confess that my own deliveries hurt like _____. I'm at a loss for words to describe it. The good news is that it was bearable—I did it! And twice completely without drugs!

For centuries before us women have been giving birth. So, if it is just fear that is causing you to pause, let me assure you that you can and will be able to make it through childbirth.

I wish I were a great writer—that the words flowed easily in order to communicate to you what it means to be a mom. It is a warm, satisfying, frightening, precious, funny, sad, inspiring, exhausting, simple, and difficult experience—nothing short of a small look inside the mind of God. There is no other relationship or circumstance that will require you to die to self more than caring for these completely dependent human beings. No other relationship will challenge your intellect as you try to stay one step ahead of them so that you can explain to these curious human being how their world works. You will desire as never before to grow in character and integrity, so that you can model for your children what those qualities look like. You will work hard to create a safe, comfortable, and nurturing environment called a home. And you will never, ever be more proud or fulfilled as a human being than when they have to write an essay on "My Hero" and they choose you or their dad.

To be perfectly honest, I also have to let you know that no

human being has the potential to cause you more disappointment, sorrow, and pain than your child. That is difficult to believe when you hold that precious bundle in your arms and feel the warmth as he or she snuggles in and you smell those wonderful baby smells. It is hard to imagine that that child could one day break your heart. Don't ever say, "No child of mine will ever…" You will surely have to eat those words in a huge serving of humble pie! (I am working on my second and third helpings right now.)

Motherhood is about joy, devotion, pride, happiness, and fulfillment. It is one of the most significant roles in a woman's life and, quite likely, the one most overstudied and least understood. Yet after the awe and wonder of the miracle of childbirth have subsided, we often do not have a clue about how this new being will affect and change our family—especially the relationship between us and our husbands. (And believe me, if you don't think childbirth is miracle, imagine carrying an eight-pound bowling ball around for nine months and then pushing it through a space not much bigger than the finger holes in that bowling ball, often without drugs and while your "loving" husband stands at your side telling you, "You're doing fine, honey.")

Several years ago, while I was the Secretary of Health and Human Resources in Virginia, it was quite popular for speakers to apply the Ashanti proverb "It takes a village to raise a child" to a whole slew of public policy issues. As the individual charged with responsibility for child welfare, social services, children's health, adoption, and other related state programs, I found this to be not only personally and professionally insulting but also a sad indictment of a culture prepared to wave the white flag of surrender in the formation and development of nuclear families.

You see, it does *not* take a village to raise a child, and no amount of compassion or empathy added to your words can make it true. What it takes to raise children are stable, intact, and loving two-parent families, *supported by the village.*

Now, just by making this statement publicly, I quickly became controversial. How could I, the child of a single mother, be so insensitive to single mothers? How could I say that two people committed to each other but not married could not offer a child the same loving environment? How could I think that the village is not involved in this? How could I ignore the reality of the new millennium and instead seem to embrace the bygone days of the fifties?

I think my own experience as a child shaped my thinking. As the only daughter in a family of six children, I watched an amazingly good and decent woman struggle to raise us on a mixture of public assistance, pitiful wages, and the kindnesses of relatives. In our case, without the emotional, physical, and financial assistance of the village—which ranged from neighbors disciplining me and my brothers before Mom got home from work, to a childless aunt and uncle taking me in and raising me when I was just five years old—we would not have made it.

Sure, you *can* raise children this way, but the toll on my mother (and millions like her) and our family was terribly difficult, lonely, and disheartening. It is not simply a question of poverty, though single mothers do represent the vast majority of the poor in the United States today.[1] Poor people are just as likely to raise good children; they share the same values, hopes, and dreams as their nonpoor counterparts. But parenting is a full-time job for two parents, and doing it alone is a Herculean task fraught with difficulty and danger.

And here's a news flash: The difference between men and women goes far beyond just the differences in our plumbing. In my opinion, raising children requires a healthy dose of what

Mom brings to the experience *and* what Dad brings. It is well documented that men and women give children different things. Indeed, one of the great advances of our time is the recognition of the critical roles fathers play in raising children. As a result, many men have spent considerable time learning about parenting and applying this knowledge. (For some remarkable resources and information about the role of fathers, contact the National Fatherhood Initiative at www.fatherhood.org.) A single parent is forced to be both mother and father, and all too often this means that neither person's contribution is effectively communicated.

The great benefit of my upbringing was that it caused me to appreciate and cherish the small, normal elements of marriage and parenthood. It not only made me work harder to understand commitment, but it also made me think about the things that I had dreamed about as a child, especially traditions and practices that symbolized what being a family meant.

Again, Edith Schaeffer had an extraordinary influence on me as I was thinking about all of this as a young wife and mother. In *What Is a Family?* she answered the title's question with this:

A family is a formation center for human relationships. The family is the place where the deep understanding that people are significant, important, worthwhile, with a purpose in life, should be learned at an early age. The family is the place where children should learn that human beings have been made in the image of God and are therefore very special in the universe.[2]

To me, the decision to have children is nothing short of an affirmation and fulfillment of God's covenant with us.

What I Wish I'd Known

Some of the things I wish I had known about children and the impact they have had on my life include the following:

Not the focus of marriage.

I wish I had known early in my marriage that children are not the central focus of a marital relationship, that I would have to work very hard not to set Charles aside. It saddens me to see young mothers ignore their husbands and devote all their time and attention to the children. If you won't pay attention to him, some woman out there will. This has practical effects on your parenting, but more important, your children will leave at some point and you don't want to find yourself sitting across from a stranger at the breakfast table. Though this is critical for the relationship between you and your spouse, many psychologists will tell you that a strong marital bond is also the best gift you could give your children.

Intensity of emotion.

I wish I had known how the intensity of every emotion, when associated with a child, is magnified. You cannot begin to understand the range of emotions children bring until you experience them. Joy, exhaustion, frustration, love, fear—all of these feelings reach new pinnacles when they involve your children. No disappointment is stronger than the emotion you feel for your child's disappointment. No accomplishment can ever cause you as much pride and joy as that of your child. The first time a boy broke up with Bizzie, it broke my heart to see her cry. When Chuck did not make the sports team he wanted, I ached for him. When Robbie got his first A, it was as if I had graduated from college all over again.

Phases are normal.

I wish I had known that I didn't have to be afraid of letting go of any particular stage, period, or phase in our children's lives; each part of a child's life unfolds as a chapter in a book. As parents, particularly mothers, we think we cannot let go of any particular stage of our child's life, but, in fact, the next stage is even better than the preceding one. I wish I had realized sooner that I was not losing something; I was simply "layering" it. Infants are precious; toddlers are cute; preschoolers are fun; and the school-age years are great. The first time the five of us had an adult evening together made me realize that each stage is as rewarding and new and alive as the previous one—and I would not give any of them up! Look forward with anticipation, not backward with regret, as your kids grow up.

Traditions are vital.

I wish I had known earlier how important traditions and memories would be for my children. I knew that they would be important for me and that we would have to work hard to develop traditions for our family, but I never realized how significant each tradition becomes for children. From my perspective, family traditions provide the strength, unity, and stability that young children need in so many ways, the familiar place to return to regularly. They are the living memory of this special unit and something that each of the children will hopefully take and share with his or her own family someday.

Though I was blessed with wonderful memories of love and values, strong and vibrant traditions were not a part of my upbringing. There is an African saying that "to go back to tradition is the first step forward." So to go forward as a family, Charles and I worked to rediscover some traditions from his family, our community, and other generations of my family, and, most importantly, to establish new James family traditions. As in many families, some of these traditions are important, such as family prayer, telling the story of each child's birth on his or her birthday, Sunday dinners, or getting the entire family together, no matter what else is happening, on the anniversary of the day four-year-old Bizzie went into cardiac and respiratory arrest (more on that in chapter 5).

Others, of course, are less significant but no less a tradition, such as everyone wearing red pajamas on Christmas Day, the annual lobster feast on New Year's Eve, and Saturday mornings with hot Krispy Kreme doughnuts.

Probably the most important was the establishment of a tradition to mark when one of our children made a public profession of faith. I was surprised to realize that some parents treated this event with nonchalance, doing nothing to mark the day. To us, it was a greater milestone in all our lives than any birthday, graduation, or wedding. Charles and I wanted the children and the rest of our family to know the value we placed on this decision, so each celebration was a little different and reflected the personality of the child involved. One was a formal luncheon after church with china and linen, another was an informal reception on Saturday evening, and the third was an intimate family dinner with a few friends. Each created a marker in our children's lives and helped them to realize how much we valued their decisions. It helped Mom and Dad during the difficult teen years to have this marker as well.

Admittedly, I personally worked on beliefs and traditions because I thought it critical for the development of my own family. The more I talk to women across America, however, the more I realize that more young couples today are struggling with building traditions as they build families. I hope it is obvious to you why it is so important to think about your beliefs now and be prepared to answer questions, teach, and share these things with your children. I hope it is equally obvious why strong traditions are part of a healthy family. Take some time today to think about your traditions, big and small, and their significance and what they convey about your values as a person and as a family.

No two are alike.

I wish I had known earlier that no two children are the same—even my own children. Though they may look alike and share many characteristics and similarities, the reality is that each child is very different. As a result, your experience and requirement as a parent to each will be quite different. There are no generic formulas or universal answers, so what works for one child could be disastrous for the next. Plan to love and discipline them as the individuals they are.

When I think about my three children, I could not imagine creating a more diverse set of personalities and challenges. Chuck is the classic older brother, easygoing and an overachiever. Bizzie is phenomenally talented at training and teaching children, though her most important priority in life seems to be thinking about what she's going to eat next, all the while maintaining a size four! And Robbie, a talented and creative thinker, perplexed and challenged his teachers because of his tendency to think "outside the box"—a gift we generally encourage. Some private testing later revealed that his IQ was higher than any other family member's, and it just took a little while longer for him to decide that he wanted to succeed in school.

Harder, not easier.

I wish I had known earlier that parenting did not get easier as the children got older. (Okay, maybe I didn't want to know this one earlier.) As a young mother, I thought—no, I was certain—that being a mother would come more easily and the challenges would be simpler as the children got older. Wrong. Just as each stage brings different and wonderful experiences, each stage of a child's development brings different and oftentimes more difficult challenges.

Early in our children's lives, Charles and I focused on behavior. As they grew up, we spent much more time developing their character and attitude. Correcting a child's behavior when he is four is easy compared to correcting a bad attitude when he is twelve, as Robbie reminded us when he reached that age.

One day in early spring 1989, Charles and I were preparing to go to New York City for a black-tie dinner, one we had been looking forward to for many weeks. I took my dress with me to work and got my hair and nails done at lunchtime. Our plan was to meet for the four o'clock shuttle and head for a very brief but much-needed getaway.

Shortly after I returned from my hair appointment, Charles called me to tell me that Robbie had been sent home from school at lunchtime for writing a bad word on a piece of paper and leaving it on his teacher's desk. After explaining the circumstances, Charles said that we could not go to New York but rather had to stay home to deal with it.

At first I objected, believing that the suspension was enough and that we would deal with it when we returned from our night out. Charles's response was one of the wisest things he has said and one that I will always remember: "If Robbie had broken his leg, we would rush home and take him to the doctor and get it set. Likewise, if he has a breach in character, it is just as important that we 'set' it right now."

Of course, we stayed home and dealt with Robbie, and though I missed our little getaway, I know we did the right thing.

One of the most helpful resources to me as a young parent, and one that continues to astound me with its relevance and resources, is the ministry of Focus on the Family. The books, tapes, and magazines on teaching and training kids provide encouragement and advice to families of all ages. When I first read Dr. James Dobson's bestseller *Dare to Discipline,* I thought he had written it for my family! (More about Focus on the Family can be found in the resource section, but you might want to check out their Web site, www.family.org, for ideas and assistance.)

Show them.

I wish I had known earlier how difficult modeling and demonstrating the proper behavior and attitude can be. Robert Fulghum, the bestselling author of *All I Really Need to Know I Learned in Kindergarten,* wisely wrote, "Don't worry that children never listen to you. Worry that they are always watching you."[3] Your grandmother was right: Children learn from what they see as well as from what you tell them. That means you need to be careful about not only what your children watch, but also what they see you watch on television; whether getting to church regularly and on time is important to you; how you react to adults who live together and are not married; and whether you treat others with respect and dignity. They will also be watching to see if you express compassion by proactively caring for the poor and the less fortunate; if you live your faith on Sundays or every day; if you put principle before expediency. You will be surprised how quickly and thoroughly your children will absorb your behavior and attitudes.

Sadly, a much more aggressive and dangerous example awaits them outside of your family. At times, the entire culture seems geared toward subverting children and challenging the values and virtues you are trying to teach them. Much has been written about the virtues and dangers of television. In our house, for a while we limited television to weekends only, and even then only for a few hours. Today there are many more channels—some are educational, but many are not. I know there are some mothers who would not be able to get anything done if they were not able to put their child in front of the television for a few minutes. But this can easily and quickly get out of hand.

Part of this means letting your children see what it means to disagree, even argue, with someone else. Your child learns how to fight from how you and your spouse handle disagreements. It is a part of marriage to disagree, but never forget the impact and influence your behavior has. Sometimes it is better to have these kind of discussions in private, but your children can also learn about civility and treating others with respect from the way you handle these times in their presence.

Spoil not.

I wish I had known earlier that it would not damage my children permanently if they didn't get everything they wanted. You can always find a good reason to spend money on kids. They are black holes that suck up money. Some parents have no ability to make the distinction between what their children need and what they want. I learned that every cent we earned could quickly get spent on schools, clothes, and toys—and still they wanted more!

One of the most dangerous habits parents can embrace is

believing that buying their children the best clothes and the best toys and the best of everything is somehow the best for their kids. It is not. Often parents will subconsciously treat their kids as things to show off. This is rooted in a sense of pride. Sometimes this pride takes the form of (again, subconsciously) saying, "I must demonstrate to the world just how big this trophy is." But children are not trophies, and this kind of response teaches your child what can easily become very destructive behavior.

God is big.

I wish I had remembered, when confronted with a seemingly impossible situation with a child, that all things are possible for God. As parents, we can make a hundred mistakes before breakfast, but God is always on the job and always a part of the equation. "All things are possible with God," we often repeat. In my own theological tradition, I believe that God has made a covenant with families. Through Scripture, I have been assured by God (I have His Word) that His children can count on His promises and a covenant of grace. This knowledge doesn't always make parenting easier, but it does mean that we have someone to walk alongside us.

The sooner you can get your hands wrapped around biblical truths, the easier you will find it to live through the times when children test you and your relationship. When you literally give your child back to God, you acknowledge that you are simply a steward and you must trust Him with the child you love so much. When confronted with a frightening situation, it is helpful to remember that God is sovereign and change is always possible. Our pastor used to remind us that God neither slumbers nor sleeps and is truly omnipotent. He is entirely capable of handling any circumstance. Therefore, if He's up, you might as well go back to bed. This can have a profound and, in many ways, calming effect on your perspective on parenting.

Open book.

I wish I had known that because of kids, my life would be an open book for everyone to share. Yes, children can thoroughly embarrass their parents, even unintentionally. One Sunday morning many years ago, Charles and I had a really vocal argument in the car on the way to church. Charles was so mad that he stopped the car, got out, and started walking home.

Determined not to let him affect my Sunday morning, I continued on to church. The children and I split up and went to our respective Sunday school classes and then into church. Unbeknownst to me, Bizzie shared our morning's journey with her class (and you can just imagine a nine-year-old's version!). At about one o'clock, the calls began. "Is everything all right, dear? Can I bring over some dinner or something?" asked one of the sweet older members of our church, to my confusion. A number of similar calls followed, some a little more prying than others.

It was not until someone mentioned "marriage problems" that I began to understand what had happened. Needless to say, the following Sunday Charles and I were in the front pew smiling and about as loving a couple as any!

Everlasting parenthood.

I wish I had known that parenthood never ends. Other women have warned me, but I think this is one that you just keep learning: Parenthood does not end when your child is eighteen or twenty-one or thirty-five. None of the events during which you might imagine your children are set free—graduations, certain birthdays, marriage—marks the end of parenting. I guess that sums up what is so wonderful and what is so difficult about being a parent.

Our roles change over the years but last a lifetime. With all of our children in their twenties, we are now advisors, encouragers, prayer warriors, financial consultants—and still Mom and Dad.

So as part of your enthusiastic planning for the future, discuss, in as deep and forthright a manner as possible, the possibilities of having and raising children. And remember that while they increase the workload in a marital relationship, they also enrich life in unspeakably wonderful ways.

Five

"Work" Versus "Career"

I knew what to expect from her even as she took a seat in the auditorium. You know the type: Her straight, blond hair perfectly combed and set, beautiful yet sensibly professional clothes, self-assured confidence.

I had agreed to speak at the spring women's forum at this Christian college, intending to discuss how women today must juggle career, family, and faith. When I called on her during the question-and-answer period, I could almost mouth the words of her question as she spoke them. "Why," she wondered, "did I get an undergraduate degree in biology and a master's degree in biochemistry to waste them staying at home as a full-time mother? I have a great, high-paying job awaiting me and a boyfriend who understands that my career is important to me, so why should I give this all up when I get married?"

I have heard just about every variation of "I'd be throwing my life away" that exists. You may not want to hear this, but I believe we can indeed have it all as women, just *not necessarily all at the same time.* The decision about whether to work outside the home or be a stay-home mom is one of the most difficult ones you and your husband will have to confront. It pits some basic drives and needs against one another, and you must be able to sort them out in a rational, realistic manner.

Today there are real opportunities for women in virtually every corner of society. As a result it has become difficult to convince women that working at home as a full-time wife and mother is an acceptable and fulfilling option.

Despite a number of studies reporting that a majority of women would actually prefer to be stay-at-home moms, we go to great lengths to deceive ourselves about this subject. Women don't seem to want honesty about this subject. Most young women know what they *want* to do, so they don't want to be confused with the *facts*.

Okay, take a deep breath. My views may run contrary to everything you've been taught by society, but let's at least try to discuss the issue rationally. People have to justify the decisions they make. As a result, many women cannot acknowledge that it might have been better for them to stay at home and raise their children. I know because that is how I started out thinking about this twenty-five years ago. It's not only acceptable; it is healthy to think through the conflicting feelings that you have about this, correct any misunderstandings you might have, and come to an understanding about what this decision means in your life and your marriage.

So if what I write makes you angry, read it and be angry. Maybe it will help you change your mind, maybe not. Maybe it will take some more thought and reading and time to come to an understanding of just what you believe.

An Old Issue with a Fresh Face

If you feel conflicted about whether or not to work, don't be dismayed. This is not a new issue; women have struggled with balancing these two options for centuries. It is clear to me, from my own background and from a study of history from biblical times to the present, that women have always worked, generally from sunrise to evening. One only has to look to the "wife of noble character" portrayed in Proverbs 31:10–31, one of my favorite readings, for evidence of that. This woman gets up before dawn, she prepares food for her family and servants, and then she goes off to conduct a number of enterprises. She works wool and flax into garments, she buys land and then plants a vineyard, and she works late into the night. Thankfully, our days are a little easier than this!

In a way, history seems to make the debate of the past twenty years seem rather moot. If you consider the periods of history when families lived on farms, you will see that women worked side by side with their husbands, whether the daily chores included crop work or canning vegetables for the winter. If you did not work, you did not eat. The same was true during the Depression and then during the world wars; women had to work to survive, and that included both inside and outside the home.

Over the years, the type of work has changed. Today we are blessed with so much freedom and luxury that we can discuss the merits of working inside or outside the home. Nonetheless, today we struggle with "work" versus "career," a distinction that I believe is subtle yet extremely important. I understand the concept of work, though I would be the first to admit that it is an old-fashioned, working-class view. I believe that work has value in and of itself. It provides sustenance; it can bestow a sense of dignity and accomplishment; it promotes the virtue of self-reliance; and it can help an individual grow in skills and knowledge.

What the word *career* means to me as a woman, however, has always been a much more difficult concept to grasp. I have met many women who have spent considerable time identifying and planning a career. I have always had a hard time comprehending five- and ten-year plans and what has to be done and in what order to get ahead. In particular, I have always taken issue with those who view politics as a career, preferring instead the notion of the "citizen-servant," especially the reluctant one who serves his country because it is the right and responsible thing to do. Public service is a noble and worthwhile endeavor, and those who have devoted their lives to either the public good or a single company are to be commended for their loyalty and commitment.

Of all the public speaking I have done in my life, the most difficult place for me to speak is at career fairs. Whenever possible, I turn these down because I find it very difficult to get my hands around "career planning." There are those who recommend self-inventories to determine career paths or surveys to discover what kinds of tasks satisfy an individual. These are totally foreign to me.

I tell those who come to me for career advice that I am the last person to whom they would want to talk. How did I prepare for the work I have done outside the home? I had no set plan or agenda other than to bring to each position a commitment to do the best work that I could, to set goals, to work to achieve them, and to treat everyone I met with civility and respect. I can easily see that we were designed as human beings to work; I am not as easily convinced that we were designed to have careers.

Why Work?

When I was involved with welfare reform in Virginia, I spent a lot of time thinking and talking about work, more so than I had ever done before. One of the elements of our plan was that individuals receiving public aid who were able-bodied and able-minded and did not have children under the age of eighteen months would work in exchange for benefits. This was a radical departure from the entitlement perspective that had been our welfare policy for the past thirty years.

Many of those who opposed welfare reform screamed about "good jobs" and "meaningful work." Somehow, they imagined that women on welfare were going to be able to go from no job to $30,000-plus career tracks. But part of the problem associated with the entitlement mentality was that they believed the recipients were somehow owed aid and any restrictions placed upon the receipt of the aid was cruel and lacked compassion. To the contrary, I often said that this kind of thinking was a kind of cruel paternalism and had diminished not only the value of work, but also the dignity and self-reliance of a generation of poor people. Indeed, these were the unintended consequences of America's misguided compassion.

To me, a good job is one that pays you fairly for your work. Work is what we do to live—it should not give us identity or define the kind of person we are. Sometimes we have to work inside the home, other times outside the home, and more and more frequently, a combination of the two.

The Fulfillment Issue

It is critical that we address the misunderstandings that many women have about the decision to work inside or outside the home, or both. The first myth about working as a full-time, stay-at-home mom is that the work is less fulfilling, satisfying, or intense than work outside the home. This is usually dispelled within days of beginning to work at home, but for those who are apprehensive about choosing working at home because of this, let me explain.

I have been involved in some pretty intense jobs in the past thirty years. Early in my adult life, when I worked at Bell

Telephone, I was involved in a program in which a business customer's phone system was replaced with another, generally one that was much larger, more sophisticated, and far more costly than the existing one. *Cutover* was the term used to describe the moment when the old system was terminated and the new one activated. Though this involved only seconds, it was critical that it be seamless, controlled, and successful, or the business could lose valuable time and information. As a result, the months prior to cutover involved intensive employee training and education, product demonstration, and investment.

For those of us involved on the phone company end of things, we knew that the cutover time and date were set and it was our responsibility to make certain that it went smoothly. This required long hours, a difficult environment, and doing whatever it took to get the job done. It was an intense atmosphere, but it was extremely satisfying to those of us involved in the work because of the great benefits to our own company and to our customers.

I have also been involved in a number of political campaigns, either for an individual or for an issue. Campaign work involves gearing up quickly for specific, often time-sensitive goals; it is intense and sometimes tense; and there are rarely any set work hours because everyone involved works marathon days. Participants have to think outside the box, stay on their toes, and be prepared for any contingency plan. Very few people thrive in this atmosphere and find fulfillment not only in the victory of their candidate or issue, but also in knowing the contribution they are making to this great nation.

I have been blessed to experience a variety of work roles, from the corporate world to the government sector to the nonprofit community. But whether it was sitting at the table discussing policy with the president of the United States or helping eliminate racism in housing, no position has ever been as fulfilling or as demanding as that of being a full-time, stay-at-home mother. Sure, there is a big change from planning a conference for five hundred to deciding between peanut butter and bologna, but the reality is that the skills, hours, and intensity required for mothering are extraordinary, and any other role pales in comparison to this one.

Consider, for instance, what is involved in the typical Thanksgiving at our house: four days with nineteen houseguests and all the laundry, cooking, cleaning, and entertainment associated with this holiday. It means a few weeks of planning, several trips to the grocery store, days of baking, and what seems like days of cleaning up afterward. Multiple flight arrivals must be coordinated, sleeping arrangements made, and everyone's personal likes and dislikes given consideration.

Give or take a few houseguests, this has been the tradition in our family for more than twenty years. I find it amusing that when I explain my Thanksgiving metaphor to men, most roll their eyes. But the skill sets and amount of work involved in Thanksgiving and on a daily basis are either the same or exceed those in work outside of the home. And for many women, this starts all over again for Christmas.

When I had a hearing before the Virginia senate for my nomination to be secretary of health, one of the senators asked me what made me think I was prepared to take this job—to manage fourteen state agencies and nineteen thousand employees. He was surprised when I responded not by applying my experience as an assistant secretary at the federal department of health and human services or my tenure as deputy drug czar, but by emphasizing that it was my role as a housewife that best prepared me for this position. You see, once you have organized a car pool, managed the sports, music, and social schedules for three teenagers, run a family, and actually managed to get by on a budget, being a cabinet secretary would not be all that challenging. Men don't want to hear that, and they certainly don't want to believe it!

The Money Issue

The second misunderstanding that many women have when they are thinking about whether to work inside or outside the home is regarding finances. Many women simply believe that they cannot afford to stay at home with their children.

We can address this issue, but first I think it is important that you know where I stand. I am as strong an advocate as you will meet for women who have the option to stay at home. There is no substitute for the love and attention that a parent can give a child on a daily basis, nor can work ever approach the significance of the moments you spend with your child.

I recognize, however, the reality that for many women this is not an option and it would be hypocritical for me not to acknowledge those women who have to work to survive. This includes single mothers and women whose husbands are disabled or are serving in the military—all of them trying to raise families in the best way they can. I know that in many families, both parents must work.

Unfortunately, those who make the case for being full-time, stay-at-home mothers often do so at the expense of these women. Would my own mother have preferred to stay at home and raise her family, rather than work from dawn to dusk cleaning other people's houses? Of course, but she never had that option.

I remember being involved in a women's Bible study in the late seventies. Our work together had focused on the role and function of women as seen from a scriptural perspective. Although the majority of these women were decent and godly women, the group discussion was basically a condemnation of those women who worked outside the home for allegedly failing in their marital responsibilities, because their children would be irreparably harmed from their lack of attention.

I thought about all of the young, black mothers I knew who did not have the option to stay at home and raise their children. Working outside the home was simply required of them for survival. For those Christian women to sit in judgment of these women seemed to me to be sadly uninformed and a small view of a mighty God. Needless to say, I left the Bible study shortly thereafter.

Having said that, I must say that I believe there is a big difference between those who genuinely *have* to work and those who simply *believe* they have to work for financial reasons. I recoil at the notion of women who can set their children and husbands aside to pursue some personal sense of fulfillment in the workplace. When the perceived need to work really has more to do with a perceived need for an SUV or name-brand clothing, I think that family should spend some time reevaluating their priorities. My counsel to young couples trying to think through the decision to work inside or outside the home is to make the decision to answer the questions honestly. Don't lie to yourself or try to justify your actions. Ask and answer: Why are you thinking about work outside the home? Will the sacrifices you make be worthy ones?

Before you say that you cannot afford to stay home, make certain that you have done the math. Most couples automatically believe that they cannot afford for the mother to stay home and raise the children. But often, working actually ends up costing them more. Consider the following example: Carole has a good job in a company with excellent benefits, earning $30,000 a year. She has one child in day care at a cost of five hundred dollars per month, which is the median cost in her community. Each month she spends eighty dollars in gas for her car, one hundred dollars to park at her job, one hundred dollars on dry cleaning, fifty dollars on lunch and snacks for her child, and another one hundred twenty dollars for lunch for herself, as well as a number of annualized costs like clothing purchases and automobile insurance.

Subtract these from her monthly take-home pay of $1,600, after taxes and benefits have been deducted, and less than five hundred dollars remains. Add another child to day care and Carole may be losing money.

I don't want to mislead you and pretend that staying home will not mean making sacrifices. Charles and I had a slightly different situation than most couples. When we had children, I was actually earning more than Charles was. But I felt so strongly about having the time with my children that I left my work in corporate America to become a full-time, stay-at-home mom. At first it was a real culture shock, and there were many times during that period when I questioned the decision. We endured years of poverty and humiliation with very little furniture or other material possessions. We had no money for maternity clothes, so I wore Charles's shirts and jeans. In place of a dining-room table, we were able to buy a wooden picnic table and benches for our dining room for less than forty dollars. This turned out to be a very practical decision, though a little embarrassing at first, and eventually it became quite a conversation piece among our family and friends.

We did not have the money to fix it up, so the house always looked like a war zone. There were no expensive dinners out and no vacations during this period. I remember one summer day when we had saved enough money to take the kids to the local amusement park. Unfortunately, we had only enough money to buy one meal, so the five of us shared that dinner. I cannot remember food that tasted as good as that fifth of a meal did then.

I would run into friends with whom I had gone to college and I could just read "poor Kay" in their eyes. But our decision was never more affirmed than the evening of December 9, 1979, when Charles and I stood next to Bizzie's bed in the Medical College of Virginia. As we held our four-year-old's hand and saw the line on her heart monitor go straight, I did not regret any of the so-called sacrifices we had made. She had been sick for a couple of weeks, and the doctors had been unable to correctly diagnose or treat her illness. We had watched helplessly as she slipped into a coma and then flat-lined. I can only imagine what it would have been like if we had arrived at that point and I had not been around to share her life with her. Who would have heard this precious three-and-a-half-year-old ask Jesus to come into her life? Who would have been there to make cookies with her and go to the zoo with her?

I wouldn't have traded one minute of our time together for any job in the world. At that painful moment, I had no misgivings about my decision to stay home and raise the children myself, no regrets, no thought of *What if I had spent more time?* We were blessed to get our baby back, but so many other mothers and fathers never do and spend a lifetime wondering about missed opportunities.

I usually grimace whenever I hear someone else say nostalgically, "Those were the best times of our lives," but I think that Charles and all of our children understand the value of those years. Not having money forced us to be creative. We were fortunate to live in the Washington metropolitan area. Our county parks were excellent and provided a mostly free source of entertainment. We visited all of the museums and monuments in Washington, many times, and taught our children about the subway system and how to get along in a big city. Because of this, our children seemed so much more cosmopolitan than many of their peers, despite being much poorer than most of them.

Some sacrifices are worth it. This one certainly was.

The Permanence Issue

A third misunderstanding concerns the permanence of this decision. Once you as a young mother make the decision to work inside or outside the home, you are not stuck with it for the rest of your marriage. Circumstances change and you may want, or genuinely need, to go back to work or stay at home at some point. I know many women, for example, who stayed at home full time until their children entered first grade. They reentered the workforce gradually, working for a few hours while their children were in school. Later, when their children were teenagers, these women began working full time again. Fortunately, as I stated in the beginning of this chapter, the skills, education, and training possessed by women today make this much easier than it was twenty years ago, as does the opportunity for lifelong learning through the Internet, community colleges, and other sources.

The Impact

There are many other misunderstandings about working inside or outside the home, some unique to your own family background. Once you make this decision, it is important that you understand what this means in your life and in your marriage.

This is an enormously important issue and one that I think

no one should decide on his or her own. Every couple should together think through, talk through, and pray through what this means. What I wish I had known when I got married was that the question of whether to work outside the home or not is a much more complex issue than I had imagined. I wish I had spent far less time feeling guilty when I had to work and far more time feeling affirmed when I stayed at home.

As she so often does, Edith Schaeffer seems to get it just right. In her book *A Celebration of Marriage* she writes:

> It seemed to me that a woman's "place" was to share the life and the work of the man she had made a choice to say "yes" to in whatever way the moment of history required, with the possibilities and diversities being endless. Farmers and their wives share the haying or the freezing of corn. The scope of going through life shoulder to shoulder in work, home and vacation, includes a variety of changing "roles."[1]

You are not always going to be certain about your decisions or happy about your sacrifices. Though we have all met individuals who find their identity in their work and are tremendously fulfilled by what they do, we are more likely to know people who have toiled in jobs to meet their responsibilities as parents. In our family, Charles was always the steadfast one, working in the same company for twenty years, often in jobs he did not like and for supervisors he did not respect. It was not always fun, or fulfilling, or easy. Nevertheless, he knew that he was providing benefits and a paycheck that were critical to our survival.

I remember a time when Charles was feeling particularly unhappy about his work situation. Some friends had come to visit us for the weekend. The husband had a great job that paid well and was very fulfilling. He spent a lot of time talking to Charles about work and strongly encouraged him to give up his present job if he was unhappy in it and find "meaningful" work, even if it meant a decrease in pay. That evening, Charles tossed and turned all through the night, thinking about these words. He thought that perhaps our friend was right, that he should quit and find something that was more satisfying.

The next morning, Charles admitted that the suggestion was very appealing. But he also realized how ridiculous and distorted this kind of thinking was. The meaning in his life was his wife and family and providing for them was not just a responsibility, but a fulfillment of that meaning. He thought of the example of his own father, working three jobs at once in order to provide for his family.

Charles possesses an old-fashioned view of work that is missing from many of today's discussions about career and work. Our parents and their parents worked as laborers. To meet their families' needs, they often worked multiple jobs, as Charles's father did. The idea of "liking your job" was a foreign concept to them. In today's new economy, we have more choices and opportunities. We have a greater opportunity to do something that is mentally and financially rewarding. If you are in a situation where you are miserable or if you have a terrible job, change it or develop a plan to do so. But that plan has to include being responsible to your family.

Again, I admit to possessing a working-class view of work. Work can be fulfilling in and of itself. But for me, work is also a sacrificial act of love for my family. That's why Charles endured jobs that were not meaningful and why I haul myself all over the country speaking. It is so much easier to sit in lonely motel rooms in far-off cities, or spend hours in airports, knowing that there is a reason for what I do. In my own case, I need to see specific results. We value education, considering it the key to lasting freedom and success. Charles and I were willing to sacrifice to educate our children, though I suspect, like many parents, we were not prepared for the "sacrifice" of supporting three kids in college at once!

Deciding to stay at home full time does not mean giving up your work habits or your commitment to excellence. We've spent so much time as a society studying time management and analyzing productivity that it would be foolish to completely dismiss all of the training that you have probably had. My kids might tell you that I was a "psycho mom," but I believed that I should approach my work at home with the same professional energy with which I had attacked my work outside the home. When I worked for the phone company, all managers had staff time and on-line time. Staff time was the time you spent in your office, reviewing your unit's work and planning upcoming efforts. On-line time was time that you actually spent on the floor managing the operators.

I applied this to my family, getting up early in the morning to have some "staff time." I planned menus, wrote out schedules for the day, made lists of things to do, and so forth. My "on-line" time was the time I spent being with the kids. Making certain that your children get the attention they deserve will require this kind of creativity and ingenuity.

The point of this information is that how you spend your time with your children is as important as how much time you have with them. I remember the women in our neighborhood who did not work outside the home who used to turn their children out early in the morning and expect them to play and be entertained until dinnertime. Children need both quality and quantity time with their parents.

Last, just because you might have decided to stay at home and raise the children, does not mean your husband is relieved of his very important role. Every man ought to be dual-tracked as well. He should be developing the skills to be a husband and father.

The Process

This is not an easy question with easy answers. But here are a few suggestions to help you figure out what is right for you and your family.

Get advice.

Seek the counsel of parents, friends, mentors, and sister-girlfriends. Get advice especially from couples whose families you respect as godly and biblically based.

Think.

Consider thoroughly issues such as child care and transportation and the costs incurred, both financially and emotionally, of both options. Try to evaluate the quality and quantity of time you will have with your children if you work inside or outside the home. Think about the positive side of delayed gratification—putting off buying that new car or the name-brand clothes or the antique rug.

Discuss.

Come to an understanding with your new husband or fiancé. Make sure you agree on this topic before you put it aside (or at least agree to disagree). It's too important to be ignored.

Maintain your skills.

Life is an uncertain journey. I have met too many women who were surprised by a spouse's death or disability or even an unexpected divorce. It is important to maintain your skills, particularly if they are affected by changes in your industry. Keep your licenses or certifications current so that if you do have to go back to work, or if you choose to, you are prepared to do so.

Be honest.

Do you *want* to work or do you *need* to work? Are you willing to turn over a major portion of the time spent shaping your child's character to a third party? Do you honestly believe that the child-care provider is just as good or better than you would be at raising your child?

This is a difficult decision. Don't rush into it, and don't shut your spouse out of your discernment process. I earnestly believe that we can have it all today: a rewarding career, a healthy and equal marriage, and a nurturing relationship with our children. But it might mean having different parts of this at different times and determining what is truly a priority to you.

Part II

After the Wedding

Six

Preventative Care

When I showed up at Phillis Brokaw's door, carrying my Bible and a bowl of fruit salad, I wasn't certain what to expect. Charles and I had been involved in Grace Church in Roanoke for nearly a month, and I was just beginning to get to know the community that would be our home. We had not found a church quickly, but once we were at Grace, everyone kept encouraging me to join this women's fellowship group that Phil hosted at her house up on the hill above the church.

I knew that I would probably be the only black woman there, though this was not a new experience for me. I also suspected that I would be the only young mother there, for many of the women's Bible groups I had seen had been made up of older women with more time for things like this.

It wasn't anything like I expected. I didn't end up being the only black woman there, though the other two women were friends I had convinced to join me. And I wasn't the only young mother there. There was a good mix of younger and older women. For many of us, this was the nicest home we had been in. The Brokaws were warm and thoughtful people whose large home reflected their commitment to family and sharing. The format was quite simple: We dropped our children off at church and proceeded up the hill to Phil's home. There, after a few moments of catching up with one another, we settled into the living room, and our hostess began teaching from the book the group had chosen to discuss. Afterward we enjoyed a potluck lunch together and then went off to retrieve our children and get back to our routines. The fellowship, teaching, and prayer was exactly the right formula to maintain me during the early, difficult years of marriage.

I believe that every woman has to take certain steps to protect and nourish her emotional, mental, and spiritual health. Just as we encourage people to see their doctors on a regular basis to prevent physical problems rather than just treat them after they occur, so too do I encourage women to take steps to insure that their roles as children of God, wives, and mothers remain vibrant and healthy.

How to Begin

Before we can take steps to maintain marital health, we need to acknowledge the threats to it. The fact is that each of our marriages is susceptible to failure. Whether because of something big or a bunch of small things, none of us is guaranteed success. Intellectually, you know that there will be good and bad days in your marriage. You might even be aware that not only might your marriage fall apart; statistically, it is likely to do so. That's the more logical side. Emotionally, however, you do not want to believe that *your* marriage will have any of those problems.

No, God will keep you and sustain your marriage, you think. You may know that nearly half of all marriages this year will fail, but I think you will be surprised to learn that the divorce rate among born-again couples is even higher than it is for the general population.[1] When they assume that God is going to keep the marriage together, many individuals do not work as hard or take their marriage seriously enough. It's as if they believe that there is some special Christian dispensation, and divorce will never happen to them. We should start our marital relationship instead with the premise that divorce can happen to each of us and then consider what that means. Prevention is always better than trying to fix something that is broken.

Either in spite of its simplicity, or because of it, the fellowship I experienced in Roanoke became one of the most influential and effective activities of my early marriage. In a single setting, I had many of the critical elements of preventative care: mentors, friends who would hold me accountable, the opportunity to learn new skills and knowledge, and the enrichment of my spiritual life.

I cannot emphasize strongly enough the importance of fellowship with other women in maintaining a healthy relationship with your husband, particularly fellowship with more experienced Christian women. In Titus, Paul stated that the older women were to "train the younger women to love their husbands and children, to be self-controlled and pure, to be busy at home, to be kind, and to be subject to their husbands so that no one will malign the word of God" (Titus 2:4–5). As I noted in the introduction, I have always found it significant that Paul chose the word *train* instead of *teach*. Clearly this is not about book knowledge; rather, the older women should take the younger women and show them how to behave.

Get a mentor.

In my own life, I have been blessed to have two incredible mentors since my days at Hampton University. I met Joyce and Beth through the campus ministry program of InterVarsity Christian

Fellowship. Since then, they have been with me every step and at every turn in my life: offering advice when it was needed, lending a sympathetic ear when I sought one, praying for and with me, and providing a little kick in the rear end when they thought it was necessary. And with the death of my mother more than ten years ago, their role in and impact on my life have become even more important to me.

There is no problem or dilemma too big or too small to share with them. Whether it concerns my relationship with Charles, raising children, or making a career decision, I can count on these women to be there for me.

Be a mentor.

Not only should every woman have mentors like Joyce and Beth, but every woman should be a "middle woman." By this I mean that every woman should be teaching a younger woman while being mentored by an older woman. Let me give you an example. You may remember Marianne, the friend who served as the wedding coordinator for Bizzie. We have known each other for nearly ten years now. During that time, she started dating her future husband, got engaged, and then married and had three beautiful children.

Maybe it's my meddling way, but we easily developed a relationship in which I was able to give her advice about dating, marriage, and motherhood. I am honored to be the godmother to her first child—a position I tell them gives me an official *right* to meddle! Whether it is the recipe for my kids' favorite tater tot casserole or a question about education, Marianne knows that she can always turn to me for advice and guidance.

A similar relationship is developing now between Marianne and Bizzie. As Bizzie encounters new ground in her marriage, she often checks with Marianne first. She calls me, too, but sometimes the advice of someone closer to your age, or outside your immediate family, is easier to take. When Bizzie begins to have children, it is likely that Marianne will be the one that she turns to with questions. In this relationship, Marianne is the middle woman, being mentored by me and mentoring Bizzie.

Church is a wonderful place to find a mentor and to find those who need to be mentored. It's important to seek women who share the same core values as you (which is why your church is a good place to look) and who model behavior that appeals to you. After that, it simply takes a willingness to listen, be honest, and be open to the possibilities God has for you, and a commitment to be in this relationship for the long haul.

Have friends.

Having friends who will hold you accountable is another critical element of preventative care. Sometimes this is more difficult than finding women to serve as mentors. I am not talking about the girls you hung around with before you got married. I'm talking about sister-girlfriends, women who will tell you that you are packing on the pounds and don't look so healthy anymore. These are the women who will tell you that you are getting lax with the discipline of your children or ask you where you were during the community Bible study last week.

It is especially easy when you have small children to become isolated. I remember how important the women I knew through Phil Brokaw's fellowship came to be in my life. Marianne has a weekly group of women who get together at each other's homes, ostensibly so that their children can play. But their time together is much more than that. It is a time for them to talk about everything from national politics to health issues to movies to their husbands. Bizzie has started a Bible study for some of the girls with whom she works. A circle of friends who share some of the same values, goals, and experiences as you will provide an invaluable support network for your marriage.

Learn more.

Learning new skills and knowledge is helpful for two reasons. First, there are times during your day as a mother that your conversation is limited to whatever your three- or four-year-old can say. The learning process—just being together with other adults—provides an opportunity for adult conversation and thinking.

Second, staying current with professional training or development will be helpful should you choose or be forced to return to work by death, disability, or divorce.

And finally, the knowledge gained through reading and studying can be incredibly useful to you in your daily life as a wife and mother. Fortunately for me, the book chosen that first year in Roanoke was Dr. Dobson's *Dare to Discipline,* which became possibly the most influential book Charles and I read as parents.

Nurture spiritual intimacy.

If you are to remain truly healthy, I strongly advise a strict regimen for spiritual nourishment. I wish I had known the depth of God's love the day I got married. Life is so different once the reality of that sinks into your core. Sometimes, the first step is simply to acknowledge that the principal relationship for each of us as Christians is with God. In a marital relationship, it is critical for both spouses to maintain and nurture this relationship, individually and together. Not only is it the best "hedge of protection," it also breeds healthiness in our relationships with each other.

Since the day Charles and I became engaged, I have prayed

for my relationship with God and asked God's protection on our marriage and family. I have also prayed for Charles and his relationship with the Lord.

Go to church.

I guess I cannot take anything for granted these days, so I should mention regular church attendance as part of your spiritual nourishment. For many couples, the last time they were in church together was the actual wedding ceremony. Don't wait until you have children, as some couples do. Become active members in a healthy faith community, particularly one with ministries for women and young adults.

What Every Relationship Needs

Gary Smalley has taught many couples to use visual word pictures to understand relationships and specific needs. For me, however, food analogies always seem to work best. I have a favorite chocolate cake recipe that is not very difficult, but it requires that you follow the directions exactly. If you do this, you will be assured the success of a rich, dark, and moist cake unlike any other.

I made this cake with some young girls who were visiting once. To make it more like a cooking show, I arranged all of the ingredients in glass bowls on the counter. There was a bowl of sugar, one of eggs, one of flour, one of unsweetened chocolate, and so on. We had the recipe. But I asked the girls their suggestions as we came to each ingredient. The girls responded differently. The sugar was good, so they thought we should put more of that into the batter. The chocolate was bitter, so less of that. And so on. When it came time to beat the batter for three hundred strokes by hand, they did not want to do that, arguing that ten strokes had mixed it all together. And baking it slowly in a low-temperature oven was just too much to ask. Turn up the heat, they said, and we could have cake sooner.

To me, enjoying a successful marriage is much like making this chocolate cake. We have all the ingredients: Some are natural and others are produced. We know the recipe for success, but so many of us do not want the work, do not want the bitter mixed in with the sweet, and certainly do not want the wait. As a result, we end up with a mess on our hands and then have the audacity to ask for a piece of cake!

When others look at a solid marriage, they often long for such a relationship. Unfortunately, not many people are willing to go through what it takes to get there. In some ways, it reminds me of the whole Y2K scare. Expecting the worst, many families and businesses spent months preparing for this New Year's Eve event, which ultimately turned out to be little more than a few isolated computer glitches.

I admit that I was one of those who became informed and interested early on and convinced most of my friends to get prepared as well. Batteries, first-aid supplies, bottled water, and canned goods were all packed tightly in our attic. In the middle of the summer prior to the big date, the weatherman announced the first possible hurricane for the season. It was then that I realized that we had been living for three years in the tidewater region of Virginia, one of the areas hardest hit annually by hurricanes, and I had never thought to prepare for what was a statistically likely occurrence. Yet I had responded to Y2K as if it were the Apocalypse itself.

That is the same way that many women, Christians in particular, prepare for problems in their marriage. They see only the worst scenario, the Y2K of relationship problems—divorce. Most women either do not believe that divorce could happen to them or know that it is really not an option because of their beliefs. The real problem often is the annual hurricane season, and for this most women are completely unprepared. I do not want to get too far off track in an analogy, but we are talking about arguments, changes, and financial or spiritual problems and their impact on your relationship.

The smart thing to do is to get prepared, to prevent problems from developing where possible, and to address those that do in a mature and rational manner. As with hurricane planning, what kinds of things can you do to insure that your relationship can sustain a direct hit?

Getting Ready for the Storms

Preventative care takes a number of forms and begins with the wedding day. Just as you change the furniture and wallpaper when you come together as a couple, so too must your habits and personalities change. Take advantage of the honeymoon period (by that I mean the first six months to a year). In Deuteronomy we are told: "If a man has recently married, he must not be sent to war or have any other duty laid on him. For one year he is to be free to stay at home and bring happiness to the wife he has married" (Deuteronomy 24:5).

During the honeymoon period, there is a tremendous amount of goodwill, trust, and a willingness to adjust. You both have a narrow window of opportunity to change bad habits in yourselves, set some ground rules, and become aware of the other's needs, strengths, and weaknesses. This is the time in which you will develop your communication patterns.

A healthy relationship with your husband requires healthy participants. Every woman can do the kinds of things that will help develop her spiritual, emotional, and intellectual health. In addition to the suggestions I have already listed, try one or more of the following:

Be a part of your church.

I've already encouraged you to find a church home. But don't just go—become a part of the community there. This will help not only your spiritual life; it will also connect you with other people who share your theology and much more. There may be an existing women's ministry that you can join. If not, perhaps you can help start one.

Join a Bible study.

Find a community Bible study or one based at your church or someone's home that is designed for women. And take it seriously: Do the homework, read the lessons, and attend the sessions. If you cannot find one, consider starting your own. There are tremendous resources available on the Web and elsewhere for this.

Take time off.

Participate in a women's night out or other opportunities to leave your children with your husband, a relative, or a baby-sitter and go out with your friends. You might do this by joining a book club, volunteering with a nonprofit organization, participating in a local political campaign, or being involved in a committee that is planning a major event. Whatever the outlet, it is important that you have some time alone and with friends.

Prevention isn't only for newlyweds, and it's never too late to begin doing these things. Just as we work to maintain and improve our physical health, so too must we work on our spiritual and emotional well-being. Though your faith should be critical to this process, don't assume that because you believe in God you are somehow exempted from storms in your marriage. You have to work on it and find friends and projects that will help keep you whole and healthy.

For me, something as simple as a neck massage or a morning at a salon can do wonders for my mental and emotional state. It may be just as simple for you: Whatever rejuvenates you, make time for it regularly. When you build the support systems for emotional and spiritual health, not only will you be preparing for the tough times ahead, but I think you will also see the benefit to your relationship with your husband almost immediately.

Seven

Uncrossing Communications

One of my favorite television shows of all time is *I Love Lucy*. There's something about old black-and-white shows; perhaps it's because they hearken back to a simpler time when humor was more important than violence. A nice, zany American girl falls in love with a suave, slightly hysterical Cuban celebrity, they get married, and the fun begins. Whether they were newlyweds living in an apartment in New York City or out in the Connecticut countryside with their son, Lucy always managed to get herself and an assortment of coconspirators into thirty minutes of trouble every week. Sometimes it was the differences in language that created the problems, but more often it was the differences in communication. She often managed to "forget" to tell Ricky something important, or she left off a critical part of a message. Other times, she simply ignored what she thought were Ricky's chauvinistic comments and did the opposite to prove something to him. And sometimes it was just pure slapstick.

Ultimately, whatever the issue, Lucy would invariably send Ricky off into a steady stream of Spanish expletives. He never seemed to learn. Just once I wanted Ricky to stop, turn to the camera, and slowly and steadily repeat the words made famous in *Cool Hand Luke:* "Lucy, what we have is a failure to communicate."

If you turn on any sitcom today, you're likely to find scenarios similar to the escapades of Lucy and Ricky Ricardo. Sometimes it is an episode based on the wife and her girlfriends doing something silly and then trying to hide it from their husbands. Or the wife says one thing but means something quite different, and then she becomes upset when the husband doesn't get it. More often than not, it's the husband who says something insensitive and the wife makes him pay for it throughout the entire show. Almost every episode of comedies today is based on either the failure of one person in a relationship to communicate to the other person or what results from two different styles of communication.

In the same way, many of the problems and even some of the funny moments in marriage (though they don't seem funny at the time) have to do with communication problems between spouses. Developing the business side of your marriage (more on that in the next chapter) is a good first step, but the really difficult and lifelong task is learning to communicate effectively with one another. I don't mind admitting that I'm still working on it. Maintaining good and healthy communications is not always easy for a husband and wife, but it is this dynamic that holds the relationship together.

Do You Speak English?

Though Charles doesn't lapse into Spanish like Ricky Ricardo, there are times when it seems that he and I speak and hear different languages. Clearly we're not alone: Not only have scores of books been written about the different styles and methods by which the sexes communicate; it seems that most of the afternoon talk shows aimed at women focus on this distinction.

In one of the most popular books, *Men Are from Mars,*

Women Are from Venus, author John Gray explains the differences between the sexes by asking us to imagine that the sexes were indeed from different planets and spoke different languages but somehow woke up here and forgot those facts. Instead of consciously trying to bridge the language differences, both sexes keep getting frustrated by their inability to communicate.

The Mars/Venus psychology reminds us of the differences God created in man and woman and what is important to each gender. Women are more relationship driven; we want to know how something "feels," and the means are just as important as the end. Men are more competitive; the bottom line is important, as is a sense of respect and a desire to accomplish something. These traits have significant impact on how we communicate as well. How often have you heard about the wife who just wanted to hear her husband say, "I love you," yet if you asked the husband, he believed that he communicated this sentiment every day? It is important to keep the differences between men and women in mind, but it is equally important to remember that people are unique. It is difficult to come up with hard-and-fast rules to ensure good communication.

I once read that on some days there are really only twenty minutes that prove critical to good communication between husband and wife. The twenty minutes were broken down into segments: the five minutes when you wake up, the five minutes before you are separated for the day, the five minutes when you reconnect, and the five minutes before bed. Can you imagine judging your relationship by these segments? If you're anything like me, it takes about an hour in the early morning before I can think coherently enough to be judged by five minutes of conversation. Charles often deals with this by bringing me a steaming cup of coffee when I first wake up—so he scores well on how he communicates in the first five minutes!

The five minutes before we're separated usually involves coordinating schedules for the next few days, figuring out what the kids are doing, arranging for car or house repairs, and banking transactions—all the things you are determined not to let your spouse forget in a single day. And the five minutes before bed? Usually I'm ready to crash early while Charles can watch several rounds of news, so it might be just a few words exchanged as we pass on the stairs.

How would your marriage be rated if I used this as a quick assessment of your communication skills? The five-minute segments seem so unimportant individually, but when you really think about it, these twenty minutes may represent the only time a husband and wife have for each other that is undisturbed by children, television, or other distractions.

The Goal of Communication

Communication is the glue that holds everything in human relationships together. It binds our hearts and souls to one another; it gives breath to the covenant we jointly make; it is our operating language, connecting us to our past, making the present possible, and envisioning the future. The goal of marital communication is intimacy. Sex may be intended for physical and emotional intimacy, but communication is intended to promote relationship intimacy. Ultimately this is important to women and men because the relationships are not independent of one another. Great communication promotes great intimacy, which promotes great sex.

Some couples try to develop "rules" for communication and to determine how they'll handle disagreements and bad moods. Sometimes this works, though I believe that more often than not it is a developed sense. There are several things that can threaten this intimacy, all of which are related to making the initial transition from being a single person to becoming part of a couple.

When you are engaged, for example, you may be used to talking to your fiancé all the time, but it is quite different once you are married and living together. I remember how Charles and I could talk for hours about any subject when we were engaged. We both looked forward to just being together and talking. Marriage changes that for many couples, partly because the mundane parts of your own life, which you probably didn't share before, are now the mundane parts of a shared life. It's easy to forget that every facet of your life is now interwoven with his. You may have been used to talking for hours about current events and politics before you were married, and now it seems that the holes in his socks are more important topics of conversation. Sometimes one spouse might think that it is inappropriate or selfish to share fears, concerns, and hopes, or even forget to do so. But that is what being a couple involves: sharing and being vulnerable and honest.

In some instances, you have to consciously work to put communicating with your spouse first, before friends and family. If you have girlfriends with whom you share everything, remember to set some boundaries. Make certain that you are not talking to them about things that you should be sharing with your husband.

The relationships with family, particularly mothers, can also threaten your ability to communicate with your spouse. I remember the first time Charles got sick after we were married. He caught the flu—sore throat, runny nose, and a fever—and just fell apart. I was all set to be his nurse—when who should show up at the front door ready to take care of her boy? Now, Charles's mother is about as dear as she can be, but when she told me that I could sleep on the sofa and that she would sleep at the foot of the bed to nurse him, I knew something was wrong! Her intentions were good and she was actually trying to help us both since I had to go to work the next day. But it was time for Charles's *wife* to assume the responsibility of taking care of her baby.

I have been blessed not to have had any issues with my own mother-in-law, but I do see the problems that mothers can create in their children's marriages all the time (yes, even—especially—me). In Genesis 2:24, it is written, "A man will leave his father and mother and be united to his wife, and they will become one flesh." You do not want to create or be put into situations where you have to choose between your husband and your mother, his mother, your sister, or your friends. If you do, however, you must choose your husband.

Elements of Communication

Communication is much more than just talk. Like any other type of communication, there are four elements in effective marital discourse: content, delivery, setting, and timing. Perhaps it is another sign of the Mars/Venus thing, but men seem to spend a lot more time thinking about the content and, sometimes, the setting of conversations. What you say is important, and where you say it can have a big impact on how it is received, but for most women, delivery and timing are far more important elements of marital communication.

Delivery is the tone or style by which you communicate the content of your conversations; timing is, of course, when you have them. I struggled for years to try to communicate how offensive Charles's tone could be at times. In marriage, the old maxim "It's not what you say, it's how you say it" may explain most disagreements and hurt. One time when Charles had said something completely benign but his tone made it the source of a morning battle, I hit upon a way to explain it to him. I call it the "sweetheart/jerk" test, although, depending upon the situation, the terms might be a little more pointed! Since then, I've used this simple test to help men and women understand how the delivery of their comments can sound to one another.

We've had many laughs as we applied these rules to our conversations. It goes something like this: If you say something to your husband or wife and, simply by the tone used, could easily add the word *sweetheart* to the end of the sentence, then your delivery is perfect. If, however, the tone of the same sentence would more appropriately call for the word *jerk* or some other insult to be added, then you can see the problem. Try it yourself on any question you might have in a given day:

> "Did you mail the bills, sweetheart?" ("Did you mail the bills, jerk?")
>
> "Did you leave the light on, sweetheart?" ("Did you leave the light on, jerk?")
>
> "Is dinner going to be ready on time, sweetheart?" And so on.

Delivery can kill whatever the impact good content intended.

Perhaps it is sensitivity to our regular hormonal changes, but women seem much more attuned to the importance of timing. Even so we can have wonderful content, delivered in the best setting with just the right tone, and still fail because we chose the wrong time to make our remarks. Don't bring up personal issues in front of the dinner guest. Don't deliver the news about the bill for the furnace when your husband is tired and hungry. Timing requires knowing the person with whom you are trying to communicate and understanding what else is going on in his life. After you learn and practice this concept, you will need a great deal of patience as your husband struggles in this area as well.

There are other forms of communication in a relationship as intimate and deep as a marriage, forms that develop between two people as the years pass. Several years ago we were having dinner at a restaurant in Richmond, Virginia, with a newly married couple. It was my favorite kind of restaurant—unpretentious, with older waitresses prone to conversation and old-fashioned, straightforward food. It was the kind of restaurant that attracts a big crowd of retired couples (perhaps for the wonderful early-bird specials), so we were easily the youngest ones there.

Seated at the table next to us was a couple whom I would guess had been married for thirty years or more. From the moment they entered the restaurant, they appeared particularly attentive to each other. But when they sat down, things seemed to change. Though they seemed to exude a mutual devotion, they did not speak to each other from the time they ordered until the time they left. After they had gone, we spent the next few minutes discussing them, wondering aloud about their circumstances and their relationship. At first we all felt sorry for them, pitying them for the silence that had permeated their time together. But as we talked about what each of us had observed, we realized that this couple had been in constant communication all the while they were in the restaurant. When he touched his plate with his knife, she passed the salt. When she looked at her glass, he asked the waiter for more water. The way he touched her arm when he put her raincoat around her shoulder, the way she rubbed the small of his back as they turned around, a nod of the head here, a small smile there—throughout their meal, they shared the comfortable communication of silence that comes only with time and understanding.

Silent communication is not all that uncommon between couples and not at all easily understandable in today's world of talk. I even saw a recent sitcom based entirely on a situation similar to my restaurant experience. In addition to what silence can communicate, there are other nonverbal ways a couple communicates. A spouse can use gestures or touch to convey many things: comfort, love, affection, pleasure, or disappointment. Likewise a small gift or a personal card can convey sentiments that might be difficult to communicate verbally.

Fighting Fair

Everyone knows this, but some don't want to believe it: You will fight with the person you love. For most of us, the idyllic romance was broken by arguing even before the wedding. Today if the stress involved in planning a wedding doesn't foster some sort of disagreement between the two of you, then you will surely find something about which to disagree shortly thereafter!

Call it what you will, arguing, fighting, or disagreeing, it is a normal part of any human relationship. The more intense the feelings for each other, the more intense the discord is likely to be. Some marital fights are merely emotions run amok, the tensions of the moment, or something caused by a bad mood or bad day. Others, however, are indicative of larger, perhaps more serious, problems. Sometimes it will take a fight or a series of fights for a couple to resolve something significant in their marriage or for one of them to change. The essayist Logan Pearsall Smith wrote in 1933, "For souls in growth, great quarrels are great emancipations."[1] Marriage is a long journey of growth, and there are bound to be some bumps on the way and, hopefully, some emancipations as well.

That doesn't mean, however, that there are no rules or that anything goes. Many experts believe that it is first whether couples address conflict and then how they do that that determines how strong and enduring a marriage will be. Every couple should develop and understand some ground rules or, to put it in another way, the "rules of engagement" for disagreeing in an acceptable manner.

Don't meet anger with anger.

Proverbs 15:1 reminds us, "A gentle answer turns away wrath, but a harsh word stirs up anger." However, recognizing that we are all sinners and that we are married to sinners, we should also remember Paul's warning to the Ephesians: "In your anger do not sin" (Ephesians 4:26).

Now Paul is a good one to remind us about this, being well known for his fiery temper. The Bible is filled with examples of anger: some paternal, some cultural, some marital. Being angry in itself is not necessarily a sin. But when it is spiteful, mean-spirited, or intended to cause real harm, then it becomes sinful. An obvious example is physical abuse.

Though anger is certainly a real part of a mature relationship, physical abuse never is. Neither spouse should respond to anger in a physical way—touching or threatening the other spouse in a harmful way—even once. I discuss this in greater detail in the chapter on abuse, but any couple experiencing abuse will need to take certain steps, possibly including counseling or separation, to insure that they are able to control their anger.

Most of us have heard that policemen consider "domestic quarrels" to be the most dangerous calls they can respond to, and every newspaper reminds us of this more frequently than we need. Sadly, in the not-too-distant past, society did not take this as seriously as it should have and often dismissed abuse as an acceptable part of marriage. Today, thankfully, we recognize that this is unacceptable behavior in any relationship, and there are thousands of programs designed to help women in crisis.

Know what is off-limits.

Perhaps the most critical of the ground rules is knowing the areas that are off-limits in fights. This is very personalized and reflects the background, personality, and perceived flaws of the individual. Anger often comes out of hurting and pain, so it is important not to focus on things that hurt your spouse when you are fighting. These include physical flaws, whether real or perceived. If your husband is fifty pounds overweight, you should avoid the mean "fat" comments or jokes. You might be able to joke about his weight or his bald spot or his big feet at certain times, but when you're fighting, you should not go there.

Other areas that should be off-limits include an individual's religious beliefs, personal or professional failures, or struggles with addiction. If you're in an interracial relationship, it is not appropriate to attack your spouse's race. If you have a master's degree in psychology and your spouse graduated only from high school, mean-spirited comments about his lack of education are not acceptable. When your comments are intended only to hurt or belittle your spouse, they are inappropriate.

Understand the family baggage.

I think that it is also critical to try to understand the baggage that each spouse brings to a relationship. This is why knowing his family is important. It helps you to know what topics are sensitive, how he relates with others he loves, and how he wants to be treated. How his parents handled conflict will have a tremendous impact on how he will handle conflict with you.

I have a friend whose father-in-law is one of those lovable, gruff, old-fashioned men. He is sturdy and reliable and has sacrificed his entire life for his family. But no matter what his wife or family asks him to do, his initial answer is almost always no. You see, this gentleman always does whatever is asked of him, no matter how difficult it is or how much of a sacrifice it requires him to make. But his initial response is always in the negative.

The reason I mention this story is because I know that his young wife was alarmed early in her marriage. She found it odd that her husband would snap a negative answer when she just raised an idea with him. Initially she was surprised and a little hurt that he seemed so unwilling to listen to her request. A few months into their own marriage, however, her husband joked about his father and how legendary and dependable his behavior was: He would first say no, then later do whatever it took to accomplish the request. Once my friend figured this out, she realized she might have to endure the brief no before her husband would really consider the request.

Obviously there are many more serious situations than this, ones that involve dysfunction and not simply an old codger's behavior. If you or your husband come from a dysfunctional family, it is likely that one of you will bring some of this dysfunction into your family as well. If this is the case, you will both have to work very hard to make certain that you minimize this kind of behavior. This may be particularly difficult in times of conflict. (If you are not certain whether or not dysfunction exists in your family or your spouse's, read some of the articles written about dysfunctional people, particularly dysfunctional adults.)

Play nice.

There are some other ground rules that might fall under your grandmother's admonition to "play nice"—most for obvious reasons. You should not curse at your spouse (or anyone, for that matter). Never make empty threats. Avoid broad and personal statements such as "You always…" or "You never…" (Any marriage guide will tell you that these are among the worst things you can say when arguing with a spouse. It suggests issues that have not been discussed or resolved.) Don't say anything in anger that you wouldn't say in conversation. Be careful about what cannot be taken back once it is said.

One idea that is particularly difficult for men to understand is that everything that's true doesn't need to be said. "This casserole tastes terrible," "That haircut makes you look like a plucked chicken," "The dress is ugly": Maybe all are true statements, but none of them need to be spoken in the heat of an argument. And "But it's true" is no defense. Remember, the truth spoken in love—not the truth spoken in anger—is the goal.

Admit that hormones make a difference.

Come on, ladies, let's be honest about this. There are times when you can have something happen to you or be said to you that it will have no effect whatsoever. You can be the iron lady. But, on occasion—especially during PMS, pregnancy, or menopause—the same thing may cause you to break down in tears or lash out in anger. The pleasant wife can find herself taking on a new persona. There are times when both husband and wife should recognize that nothing good can come out of a conversation.

Some women (obviously not you or me!) can be edgy, depressed, angry, weepy, or grumpy, and, despite our best intent, these emotions can have much more to do with our communication than logic or anything else. As women, we should remember the impact hormonal changes can have on our moods and stamina.

And our husbands should remember the same thing and demonstrate a capacity for empathy.

Learn to Communicate Early and Well

There are a number of important topics I think couples should communicate early in their marriages, some of which I have discussed elsewhere in this book. Generally, anything that is significant to one partner should be discussed and resolved if possible. For instance, if husband and wife are from different denominations, they should talk about how they will handle the differences now and when children arrive. For many couples, how to handle holidays looks more like a major union negotiation than simply deciding whose parents get to cook the turkey. For others, discussing money and how they will make spending decisions is one of those important early discussions. How to discipline children is another.

Remember that how you and your spouse communicate will affect not only your relationship; it will also have an extraordinary impact on your children. From you they will absorb word choice and inflection. They will develop attitudes and thought processes. They will learn about treating people with dignity and respect. They will learn how to fight, how to handle conflict, and how to resolve differences. And, probably the most important lesson, they will learn perseverance: walking through conflict, not giving up, staying at the table, and staying in the relationship.

Use Paper If Necessary

As I mentioned in an earlier chapter, I was recently reading a copy of Nancy Reagan's book of letters from her husband, entitled *I Love You, Ronnie.* No matter what your political persuasion, it is a remarkable look inside a very famous, yet intensely private, love affair that has spanned nearly half a century. I believe that these letters offer a glimpse into the person of Ronald Reagan, but what I found myself thinking about was what they meant to Nancy Reagan. It's helpful for all of us to remember how significant the written word can be, especially in this age of pagers, voice mail, and e-mail.

While looking for something in a storage closet recently, I found a box of notes and letters from Charles that dated back more than twenty-five years. Whether it was a simple "I love you" scrawled across a card or a longer letter, these notes serve as a marker of something that existed at a certain time and that has grown even stronger. They are something I can go back to for strength, whether just for a warm chuckle or a quiet tear. For Nancy Reagan, struggling to care for a husband whose memories have been erased, letters are a marker to go back to for the warm glow of a better time.

Not everyone is a great communicator and it is not always easy for spouses to communicate intense feelings. Sometimes you have to work just to make sure that you do talk. For Ronald Reagan, who certainly was affected by the failure of his first marriage, that meant writing to Nancy no matter how far apart they were or how significant the things that competed for his attention. With our hectic lives, Charles and I used to have "raisins and nuts" evenings as a way to structure time to communicate. I would get all the kids into bed early and set out some bowls of raisins and nuts and other snacks (okay, so it was during my health-food stage) in the living room. For the next two hours we would talk about anything—the kids, work, families, dreams, fears, and prayers. Today, with even busier lives and hundreds of channels on the television, it might be easy to miss these special times together.

Creating an environment for good communication might include one or more of the following:

Start your own.

Create your own "raisins and nuts" evenings. If you have kids, put them in bed early, build a fire, prepare some snacks, and spend an hour or two together—without the television or telephone to distract you.

Get together.

When you go out, don't always pick movies or dinners with friends where your one-on-one time will be limited. Go to a coffee shop or bookstore and talk—about anything.

Melt anger.

Remember the warning in Ephesians 4:26: "Do not let the sun go down while you are still angry." If something is bothering you, don't get into the bed, yank at the covers, and hug your side of the mattress. Try to talk about it in a calm manner. If you do go to bed angry, try to understand *why* you are angry and agree to talk later.

Make minutes count.

Think about those five-minute segments that sometimes comprise all of the communication you have with your spouse. Do you make the most of them? Are the five minutes spent in a meaningful way or not?

Communication is a huge part of your marriage, but that doesn't mean you can't address it in small but meaningful ways. Good communication between spouses will improve every other aspect of marriage: everyday life, parenting, finances, sex. And the most important thing to remember is not that you have to agree on everything—you won't—but that you are willing and able to discuss and live with your disagreements and irreconcilable differences. Don't try to hide conflict; embrace it in a loving, Christian manner, and you will do wonders for your relationship.

Eight

Financial Foibles

I t never failed. Our checking account was perilously close to zero, and payday was a week away. We needed food for the kids and gas for the car, but there was no cash until the paycheck came. Besides, a stack of bills teetering on the counter awaited that money. This didn't even take into account the things we thought we needed, like school clothes for the children.

I knew I would be up and worrying every night. Charles, on the other hand, would be lying next to me, sleeping like a baby and unaffected by what I thought was our imminent financial ruin. This is not necessarily a husband/wife distinction, but each spouse views money and is affected by financial problems differently. In our family, it is Charles who has had what seemed to be a cavalier attitude about money. It is never a big deal to Charles. If we have it, great. If we lose it or don't have it, no big deal— we'll earn more soon. I am the one who worries about the next grocery trip or tuition payment or a late notice from the gas company. So, early in our marriage, we usually ended up with me getting angry at him for his recklessness and lack of interest and Charles being confused by my apparent unwillingness to trust God.

If you are engaged or just married, you may not yet know something that every married couple soon learns: *Money is always an important issue in marriage.* Everything may be going great—you may be off to a wonderful and well-thought-out life together—but nevertheless you might still be headed for disaster. As on the *Titanic,* however, one small navigational change could save the ship.

I'm talking about the business side of being married. Make no mistake about it; what you've started is a business, in addition to everything else it is. No, it's not Wal-Mart, but it is a small family business in every sense of the word. For instance, in the communication chapter we discussed how you treat each other and how you resolve conflict—sort of the personnel policies and grievance process for your family.

Like any other small business owner, you have to be prepared to nurture and care for this enterprise. Often when businesses fail, it isn't because the service was not good, or because the owners didn't have a good product. Consider all of the great restaurants that start and fail in your community in a year. It's rarely because the food was bad, or the service was inadequate, or the atmosphere was unpleasant. No, the owners thought those issues through with great care and attention to detail. What they probably didn't do was apply the same attention to the business aspects of their restaurant—paying employee taxes, taking care of vendor bills on time, reinvesting profits into the business. Some people can have a really good idea but fail because they do not have a business plan or business manager in place.

Start Now

The engagement period is a good time to think through the business aspects of marriage, to talk about how you will handle money and which spouse will be responsible for what. If you didn't do it then, start now. Let me address one of the first mistakes many couples make today right off the bat. If you set up separate bank accounts—thinking *my money* versus *his money*—expect problems. A lot has changed since women began working and achieving a certain amount of financial independence. No longer do we need men to "make it" financially. Notwithstanding that, when the Bible says that a man will "be united to his wife, and they will become one flesh" (Genesis 2:24), it doesn't list an exception for "separate bank accounts."

Let's be honest here. If you don't trust him with "your" money, can you really trust him with your emotions, your physical well-being, your children, and so forth? When you set up individual bank accounts and separate "my" bills from "your" bills, you acknowledge one of several things. You're saying: *I don't think this relationship is going to last; I don't trust my fiancé; I married someone I don't respect; I will give him my body but not my cash.* If that's the case, the separate accounts are symptomatic of a larger issue, and you can go ahead and skip to the chapter on crisis points. Marriage means that you take on each other's strengths and weaknesses, assets and liabilities. Remember the saying "What's mine is yours and what's yours is mine"?

Again, the engagement period is a good time to resolve any differences regarding finances and to prepare for life after the wedding day. It is also the time in which both people must be honest about their finances. There shouldn't be any surprises after the wedding. If you owe a lot in student loans, credit card bills, or something else, don't wait to surprise your husband with the debt you are bringing to the marriage. Likewise, if you have saved a lot of money or have a stock portfolio or own real estate, share the information before you get married. (If you didn't, share now!)

For some couples, the groom-to-be or new husband begins to

set up a financial system during the engagement period or immediately after the honeymoon. It certainly doesn't have to be the groom's responsibility, but this is a great arrangement prior to the wedding—as long as you do not disengage completely from the process—because it allows you to focus on the logistical arrangements for the ceremony with the confidence that your finances and other administrative changes are being addressed. Otherwise you will be dismayed by the amount of time you will both have to take after the wedding to make all of the changes required, from changing addresses and names to transferring bills and combining accounts.

I am certain that this is one area where engaged or newly married couples underestimate the time and frustration involved in "becoming one." If you don't think the government is bureaucratic now, just wait until you try to file your taxes jointly and the government does not recognize your new name! A simple way to start is to go to the office supply store and stock up on things that will help you merge your financial lives. Set up a system for your future together before the wedding takes place!

When Charles and I were first married, these huge office supply stores were few and far between, but today office megastores can be found in almost every community. We can easily spend an hour or so in the aisles there, looking for new filing systems and organizers for our home. The hard part then becomes scheduling the time to implement our systems.

Taken alone, each of these suggestions seems relatively unimportant, but I can assure you that setting up systems and processes regarding your finances is one of the most important steps in a marriage. Getting married is very much like setting up a small office. You have to agree on joint files, establish bookkeeping methods, develop a budget after determining revenue and expenses, and be accountable for your responsibilities.

I cannot tell you what kinds of systems and processes will work best for you. There are hundreds of good books available that focus exclusively on this, even whole sections at many Christian bookstores. In establishing our philosophy and setting up the James family system, we have used a lot of recommendations made by two excellent Christian financial advisors, Ron Blue and Larry Burkett. My only point is that you should find whatever works for you and make the decision to start it and stick to it. It might be something simple, like three-ring binders with a tab for each month, the filing system we started with. Or it might be an electronic system, like Quicken, which we use now. Everything is computerized, and we can now print out reports, logs, registers, and forecasts (and we regularly back up our systems on disk). Your system for tracking expenses may rest somewhere between either paper or computers. I am a great advocate for on-line payment systems; the time saved and the stress reduced will be worth the initial time spent starting up.

You should also establish some rules of finance before you get married. It makes an enormous difference if you've proactively determined not only where the money goes, but also how you will decide to spend savings, make financial decisions, and plan for the future. If you're reading this two months into your marriage (or even two years) and you haven't done so yet, don't despair. It is not impossible to do it now; it just requires overcoming some habits that you might have gotten used to since you were first married. Go ahead, take the plunge—go all out and buy the supplies. Color code the file folders, set up the systems, agree on the shared duties, and implement your plan together. You might be surprised how fixing the business side of your marriage will reinvigorate other parts as well.

Money and Friends

One of the few things almost guaranteed to cause problems in a marriage concerns friends and lending money. I think Ben Franklin had it right when he wrote, "Neither a lender nor a borrower be." Whether it is a friend or a relative, being asked for money brings on all kinds of problematic issues. Many women have told me about finding out that their husband had lent money to a friend without telling them, or that they had secretly borrowed money from a sister and still couldn't pay her back. Sadly, money often begets secrets that can do real damage to a relationship.

In our family, we have a hard-and-fast rule: no loans and no cosigning for loans. That goes for children and other family members as well as for friends and neighbors. If a friend or relative needs money, we try to give it to them either with no strings attached or with the knowledge that we do not expect to be paid back. I'd rather pay for something directly or give someone money than take the problems that come with loans. (We have also been careful about borrowing money from friends and family. On those few occasions when we did, it was always from a parent or close friend that we knew could go without the funds until we were able to pay the money back. And then we made repaying the loan our priority.) We didn't just come up with this rule; it unfortunately took a few painful experiences for us to get to this point.

Once we had seven hundred dollars saved—a huge amount for us in the first year of marriage. Though it had taken a long time and been really difficult scrimping and saving to get that amount, it felt great to know that we had a little cushion in the bank. Naturally, right around that time, we received a call from a friend who was facing a financial crisis. He needed a lot of money immediately, but he was certain that paying us back wouldn't be a problem because he would get paid in a couple of days. If we could loan him some money to cover his shortfall, he would pay us right back. Charles and I discussed it and, taking him at his word, sent him a check for seven hundred dollars.

We breathed a little easier when, as promised, he mailed us a check a few days later for the full amount we had loaned him. Rather than put the money back into our savings account, though, we decided that we would deposit it in our checking account and go ahead and pay off some bills. A day later, we wrote seven hundred dollars' worth of checks to reduce various debts.

As you may have already guessed, our friend's check bounced. Since we didn't have any extra money in our checking account, all of the checks we had written followed suit. Not only did we have to pay the fees associated with bad checks, we had to pay the amounts for which we had written checks. As a result, we had to borrow nine hundred dollars from Charles's parents, a loan that took us years to repay.

From this and other experiences we realized that if we could not afford to give it away as a gift then we should not loan money to anyone. The relationships we have with family and friends are more important than money. If a friend or relative defaults on a loan or you have an expectation that you will be repaid by a certain date and you are not, it can destroy the relationship. It was not only beneficial for Charles and me to come to an agreement on this, but just having a clear policy in place has also discouraged us from getting involved inappropriately in other people's problems.

Money Priorities

All money is not equal when it comes to setting priorities for spending. When you have a set income, you make a budget and live within it (or at least you should). In doing so, certain things take precedence over others. This theory is neither original to me, having both historical and biblical roots, nor is it rocket science. Nevertheless, despite such common knowledge, few couples seem to get it right. In talking to Christian women, I hear the same message over and over again: They trust God with their lives, but they'll manage their own money!

For me, the biblical principles of money management seem clear: first tithing, then debt reduction, then saving, and finally investing. Commitment to this technique requires one thing that a lot of us seem to lack: a great deal of faith. We don't want to trust God when it comes to our salary or when we have to give 10 percent of our income back to kingdom work. What role does your faith really play when it comes to finances?

Let's look at these steps one by one.

Tithing.

Melchizedek king of Salem brought out bread and wine. He was priest of God Most High, and he blessed Abram, saying,
"Blessed be Abram by God Most High,
Creator of heaven and earth.
And blessed be God Most High,
who delivered your enemies into your hand."
Then Abram gave him a tenth of everything.

GENESIS 14:18–20

Let's get real honest here: If you are not tithing, why exactly aren't you? I think our responsibility as Christians is clear. Some debate whether we should give 10 percent of our gross or our net income back to God. Some argue whether it must be given to the church or to any Christian endeavor. Very few Christians will argue that tithing is not a biblical mandate, but we have every excuse in the book why we can't do it. How many excuses can you come up with for your own situation? *We can't afford it right now. When we get a raise, we'll use it for tithing. We have too much debt.* Keep going, I'll bet you can come up with others that you might have heard in your own family!

I know this is a difficult concept to undertake if you haven't been doing it all along. But if you really believe what Scripture says, then you need to consider whether disobedience of God's Word is caused by selfishness or a lack of faith. Instead of praying for more money, we should be praying to be obedient to His Word and for an increase in faith. Making tithing a priority is sometimes difficult—like any new habit, it takes discipline. It doesn't require faith to "inch up" to 10 percent; it requires faith to actually begin today to pay 10 percent.

Further, our failure to tithe is often not caused by a lack of money, but rather a lack of commitment to the principle itself. Tithing forces us to set priorities. If you have limited income, tithing forces you to cut out certain other things, perhaps things that weren't needed or shouldn't be priorities after all. If you figure out your tithe and don't have enough money for car payments or credit card debt, perhaps you have incurred too much debt. (In this case, you need to try to meet both priorities—tithing and debt reduction—and work to eliminate the latter as quickly as possible.) God knows the truth, so we might as well admit it to ourselves and work to make Him and His work a priority in our lives. He chastises us about robbing Him (Malachi 3:8–12), yet we continue to do so.

I recognize that this is hard if you are not already doing it—tithing and trusting. But you must trust God and His ability to meet your needs. Again, like any new habit, it gets easier the more you do it!

Debt reduction.

Let's keep it real *and* simple: Credit cards can ruin your life! They promise to give you self-esteem, entreating you with letters proclaiming your "credit worthiness." The credit companies write to you even before you graduate from college, telling you that credit cards are the keys to independence. They ply you with offers of low interest, bonus points, and frequent-flyer miles. What they neglect to tell you about are annual fees and interest rates or that you will probably be paying for things long after you use them and throw them out.

Credit cards are mild in comparison to store charge cards. Stores lure you with offers like 10 percent off your initial purchases but forget to tell you about interest rates of 21 percent—rates that quickly cancel out the up-front discount for using the charge card.

For our first Christmas together, Charles and I spent a lot of time thinking about presents for our family. We didn't want to purchase anything excessive, just something simple and thoughtful for each person. A red robe from Sears for Charles's mother. A bottle of a nice cologne for his father. A set of sheets from J. C. Penney for his sister and her husband. A portable radio for my brother. Warm slippers and a sweater for my mother.

It was a good year, but the following Christmas, we realized that we couldn't afford to buy anything for our family because we were still paying for the previous year's presents.

It's a good idea to have a credit card and an even better idea to reserve it for emergencies. At one point, Charles and I had a charge card for virtually every store in Richmond. As soon as we were able, we got rid of the store charge cards and used cash as much as possible. We found that we actually spent less when operating on a cash basis. Today we try to reserve debt for the big, essential things: cars, homes, and tuition. Looking back, we realize that if we had used cash instead of charge cards years ago, we could be paying cash for some big things now.

When you are determining where and how to spend your income, reducing debt should be a very high priority. Of course, we all know that debt would not be a problem if we didn't incur it, but somehow we all seem to end up with any number of credit and charge cards. Charles and I made debt reduction a priority one year, and we determined that after tithing we were going to use every spare dollar to get rid of the debt we had accumulated. I made up a list of every card and the balance owed and posted it on the refrigerator. At first it was a little depressing. I would go to get an apple and be reminded how poor we were! But after a few months it became exhilarating to know that we were finally breaking free of debt. We actually were able to get rid of it in less than a year.

Unfortunately, as with any recovery program, you sometimes have to try it a few times before you get it right! We didn't get rid of the cards; they sat in our wallets with zero balances for a few months. Then our old habits began to creep back in. Within eighteen months to two years, we were right back where we were before. This time we knew to get rid of the cards. Keep only a general credit card and reserve it for emergencies that are beyond your savings.

I know what debt is and what it can do to a marriage. The struggle to break free can become all-consuming. Recognize your own limitations, and, if you cannot get out on your own, contact the Consumer Credit Counseling office in your area or another program that helps you eliminate debt and manage your finances based upon biblical principles.

Saving.

I have a friend—a young, well-educated, professional black woman—who told me about taking a recent trip down South to visit her mother. While she was there, she thought it important that they discuss her mother's financial situation, in part because she was nervous about what would happen to her mother as she got older and the impact this would have on her own financial situation. To her surprise, this poorly educated old woman possessed a rather substantial financial portfolio that included cash, stocks, and property far exceeding my friend's net worth. It was almost impossible for my friend to believe how her mother could have built up such assets when she had earned only minimal income from low-paying jobs.

My friend's mother's strategy is neither new nor revolutionary. It's a well-kept secret entitled "Compound Interest Can Change Your Life." Young people today don't seem to understand it, particularly with the flashy promises of quick-and-easy fortunes through the stock market or the state lottery. But most Depression and post-Depression families do: The combination of delayed gratification, thrift, and compound interest can do more to provide long-term financial stability than any dot-com stock offering.

We used to have a little game we would play with the kids to teach them about compound interest. We would give each of them a penny. A week later, we would give them another penny if they still had the first one. The next day or week, we would give them an additional penny. After a few weeks, they could see how dramatically their savings had grown. Then, when we explained what banks were for and what happened to savings if they kept adding to them and left them there for the long haul, they were genuinely excited about saving.

Delayed gratification is a concept practically alien in today's culture. We are all conditioned to believe that we deserve everything we want when we want it. We want to buy new clothes every season. We want to get a new car every couple of years. Our kids wear sneakers that cost more than my monthly food budget did when I was a young mother. Women of the Depression used to have a motto: "Make it last, use it up, wear it out."

Being thrifty could be roughly defined as being able to save something regardless of circumstances. It means buying ice cream on sale, if at all. It means squirreling away a dollar here and a dollar there. Saving could be for a short-term need like a car or a needed improvement to your house. Or it could be for something further down the road, like retirement or catastrophic illness. And when you save that money in a bank for a long time, that is when the miracle of compound interest begins to bear fruit.

One year I found myself seated next to Ron Blue at the NCAA Final Four basketball tournament. Charles has an entire shelf of Ron's books in our home office and has listened to every tape or radio interview possible. Knowing that he would be very disappointed if I didn't get some advice from this financial genius, I asked Ron to give me some profound financial tip to impress my husband with. Without even cracking a smile, he said, "Spend less than you earn."

I laughed and said, "No, seriously."

He was quite serious. And even though this was a lesson Charles and I learned the hard way, it amazes me today to learn about the number of couples who are not able to understand this concept and find themselves in financial trouble as a result.

I did not know what broke was until I got married. There's something liberating about being a single woman, working and making a paycheck. Then something happens when you get married and later when children enter the picture. I wish I had spent more time as a single woman figuring out finances, money management, and how to stretch the dollar. Whether it is buying things on sale, in bulk, or at the cooperative, using the public library for books and videos, making handmade gifts, or looking for free entertainment, there are numerous ways to do this and still meet the needs of your family.

One warning: Be careful of the false economies of scale. Often families struggling on a budget will see a wonderful deal and think they are saving money by stocking up on a particular item. Though this might work in some cases, a lot of cupboards are filled with cans that go unused for years. I know one husband who buys pancake mix on sale every time he does the grocery shopping. This family has enough pancake mix to supply their community in the event of a famine!

I also wish I had known earlier that it's easier to be responsible about money if you never get the cash in your hands. Direct deposit and automatic deductions have revolutionized my life. When we got the money directly and were responsible for using it to pay the bills and save, all kinds of things competed for what seemed to be such a small amount. But once it went right into the bank and we used an on-line bill-paying service, my perspective of money changed. Even the government realizes the effectiveness of immediately sending your hard-earned funds into their accounts. This is why federal and state governments use withholding methods to deduct various taxes prior to the deposit of your money into your accounts.

A simple fact to remember is that poor people who manage their money well often have more disposable income than their middle-class counterparts who manage poorly.

Investing.

In today's financial and stock market environment, it is difficult to resist the urge to invest and attempt to make a quick buck.

Everyone's doing it, it seems, particularly all those smart people who got in on the dot-com start-ups. The Internet has spawned an entire generation of day traders.

Regardless of who in your relationship wants to start investing, it is important that you do this only at the appropriate time. There are a lot of other spending and saving priorities that must come before investing; in fact, it may be years before you can get to it. For us, nearly twenty years passed before we had money for anything other than a crisis or tuition payments. I recently met a mature, well-off Christian couple who told me that it wasn't until their children had graduated from college that they were even able to begin saving, and investing came even later.

The recent demise of so many dot-coms and the radical fluctuation of the equities market is a good reminder that however well informed your activity, investing is still based on some level of risk. Should you invest? Absolutely, but only if a loss does not affect your other priorities such as tithes, debt reduction, savings, or living expenses.

Just in Case

Early in my marriage I learned a very practical financial tip from an unexpected source: the pioneer women in old western movies. Typically when the crops failed or were destroyed, the wife went out into the cornfield or behind the chimney and came back with a dirty sock full of cash. She always had some money set aside that would save the day. And it's true today, too: Every good woman worth her salt has some money put aside for a rainy day—a "stash."

I figured this out in the days when we didn't have two nickels to rub together and have always been amazed at what strong women can do: We can figure out how to feed the family and skim a little out of the budget. It's money put aside not for personal reasons, but for the family. In the early days, when the phone bill was getting backed up or when Charles said there wasn't enough money for us to buy that very special birthday present or make an emergency car repair, it was so good to be able to say, "Honey, let me go back in the bedroom for a minute and see what I can do." He knew the stash was for us, for our family. I realized keeping a stash was a skill of a Proverbs 31 woman, an essential one if I wanted to be prepared for an unpredictable economy.

Since then, I have always had a stash. I just wish that I had figured this out earlier and that I had learned it from a godly Christian woman instead of a western movie. No one shared this important lesson with me, and that is precisely why I am telling you. (Some women have told me that their husbands are control freaks and would be livid if they knew their wives were doing this. In this case, I would probably avoid keeping a stash, but these women have far more serious issues about control, "his" money and "her" money, and communications.)

Another good—in fact, invaluable—idea is life insurance. I already knew this, being raised by an insurance man. My husband, having learned from his father's example, knew it also. In order to protect your spouse and children, life insurance is an essential safety net. And the more children you have, the more life insurance you need to replace the income of the primary income producer in the event of an accidental death or other tragedy. The cost of raising a child is considerable, and an unexpected death often forces the surviving spouse back into the workforce or, for those already working, adds the pressure of working another job to provide for the family.

Adequate insurance coverage provides your family with security to maintain a home, albeit perhaps not the same home, and some means of income or savings for those who are left behind. I encourage you to purchase insurance before the honeymoon or at least before the first child. Talk to an established agent and learn the differences between term and whole policies, then decide what is right for you. As your family grows, make certain that you increase the amount of coverage.

In addition, be certain that you have disability insurance. We generally remember to get insurance on our lives, homes, cars, and property, but we often forget one of the most basic things: our income. Disability insurance is a small investment to insure that your basic needs are met and to safeguard your ability to pay your mortgage and medical bills should the need arise.

Though it may seem to be years down the road, every woman (and man) should eventually have a long-term care policy. With today's medical advances, there is a far greater chance that I will spend time in a nursing home than the chance that my house will burn down. Yet many families have insurance against fire but no plans for the care they might need later in life. I think this is one of the best gifts we can give our children. We often wondered early in our marriage why we didn't have as much disposable income as some of our friends. Tithing, debt reduction, savings, and insurance payments accounted for that. As the years unfolded, our early decisions proved to be good ones.

When I think about everything I have learned about money and finances, I realize that much of this is actually what I wish I had learned as a child about the value of money: delayed gratification, the importance of savings, trusting God when it comes to finances. In the past twenty-eight years, we have grown tremendously in our relationship and in our knowledge of the financial acumen required to run this business called a family.

When you have your first argument about finances or face your first financial crisis as a couple, don't be discouraged. It is possibly the most common source of friction in a relationship. Remember your own money priorities, trust God, and learn from your situation.

Nine

Intimacy Versus Sex

I get up at 5 A.M. to start the twins' first feeding. I make breakfasts, pack lunches, and drive the car pool. When I get home, I clean the house, do two loads of laundry, and try unsuccessfully to stay ahead of the mess the kids make every time they play. Then it's time for dinner and baths and bedtime. When I go to bed at night, I am exhausted, sometimes frustrated, and always preoccupied with whatever is going on in the lives of the kids. All I want to do is sleep! I guess if I were honest I would admit that my T-shirt and faded gym shorts send a message to my husband: *Honey, stay on your side of the bed, and keep your hands off of me!*

I must admit that I was taken aback when I first heard these words at my hair salon. Though I understood her feelings of exhaustion and stress, this young mother of four children (the youngest were twin boys) surprised me with her quick and honest response to my question. For several years now, I have been collecting material for this book. Wherever two or more women were gathered, you could count on me to throw out the question, "What do you wish you had known about earlier in your marriage?" It is perhaps no surprise that sex came up most often as the topic of conversation.

In today's sex-laden culture, that confused me. Information and graphic details are everywhere: movies, books, magazine articles, and song lyrics. So why are so many women confused, mystified, surprised, disappointed, or uninformed about the sexual relationships they experience with their husbands? I believe that the answer is because there is a big gap between the perception and the reality of sexual relations in pop culture today. A gap between what the world proclaims and what God intended. What she expects and what he expects. What she thinks and feels and what she expresses to her spouse. The short answer is that if you can lessen the gap in all these areas, you are well on your way to a better sex life.

Sex is a critical element of a healthy marriage. Ask any man, and he will say "amen!" Ask any woman, and she may or may not agree. Not surprisingly, it is also the source of many of the problems couples face, particularly in the first few years.

By the way, there is nothing wrong or inappropriate or unrealistic about what the young mother said. I've heard these sentiments expressed in different ways by hundreds of women. We *are* exhausted and stressed out and seem to have lost interest in sex (except on rare occasions) and can't figure out why that's all that's on his mind. One woman told me that her husband had been very sick for several days. After caring for the kids and nursing a sick husband all day (and we all know how trying that part can be!), she finally retreated to the bathroom for a hot shower to end a long and exhausting day. As she walked from the bathroom to her lingerie drawer, she noticed him watching her as she put on her nightgown. By the time she climbed into bed, he was ready. Thus ensued the following dialogue:

She: "But honey, you're sick."

He: "But, sweetheart, I'm not dead!"

Elements of Great Sex

More than a decade ago, I spoke frequently in high schools. The topic "How to Have Great Sex" always garnered a great deal of attention. Somehow the novelty of this conservative Christian woman coming to speak to high-school students on this subject sparked a lot of interest in both students and faculty. I would always start by telling them that I thought that sex was great and that I enjoyed it and found it fun, exciting, and fulfilling, both emotionally and physically.

Then I would ask the students to talk through what they perceived the elements of great sex to be. "We've all decided that 'great sex' is something we want," I told them, "so let's figure out how to get it."

We'd always start with the tangible element first: a great place. Where do we want to have sex? Someplace safe, comfortable, conducive. The back of a car is not a good place (too cramped and uncomfortable). Your bedroom in your parents' house is another bad choice (not private and someone might come in). A cheap motel does not make for romance (stale smells and flimsy, used sheets). Now while all of this may be important to women, to men, all of the places listed might not only be acceptable, but also might be exciting! Each woman's idea of the "right" place might differ, but finding it is one of the necessary elements of great sex.

Another element of great sex is timing. By this I mean two things. First, we want sex to occur at the right time. We want to be emotionally and physically interested in it. Being emotionally ready involves many factors—things such as trust, commitment, confidence, security. And second, we want it to be leisurely; we don't want to be rushed. "Hurry up and let's do it before someone catches us" are hardly romantic words in anyone's language.

A final element, and the most important, is the right person. What do you need from this person? He has to be someone who cares deeply about you, not just about having sex with you—though he should want that, too. He has to be there for you and be interested in pleasing you. You want him to have your best interest and pleasure as priorities. He has to be committed—really and truly committed—to you and your relationship. And, of course, you don't want to worry about diseases or about being abused or being hurt.

When you brought all these elements together—the right location, the right time, and the right person—truly great sex could follow. And interestingly, at the end of this discussion, almost every student agreed that great sex was best achieved through a monogamous relationship within marriage.

This revelation seems contrary to much of the prevailing thought among women today. In popular culture, sex is for fun, entertainment, and meeting "my" needs. We hear this repeated in movies, on television, in songs, and in conversation among young and old, rich and poor, black and white. "I have my needs." "My priorities must be met first." Sadly, this often translates into many women pursuing elusive and unrealistic goals—trying everything and ending up frustrated and lonely.

As married women, we still find these elements to be very critical. Marriage is the environment in which great sex can occur. I would be bold enough to assert as well that it is the only environment for great, world-class, top-of-the-line, extraordinary sex! Why settle for anything less?

The Script Has Been Flipped

I noticed a cultural change recently when I went to see the movie *The Brothers*. This film focused on the lives, particularly the "relationships," of four men. In the movie, the lead character meets a girl in the park and a few hours later they are in bed laughing over who is the real "slut puppy." There was a time when if a guy had sex on the first date, it was acceptable, while a girl would be trashy to do the same. Now it seems that neither is a "slut puppy," that it is all right for men and women to act like barnyard animals!

Both in movies and in real life, it used to be that the relationship preceded the sex. Couples courted and spent a considerable amount of time getting to know each other *before* they had sex. Today the reverse is true. A relationship may or may not evolve from the sex. Sex is a casual encounter and often occurs within hours or days of the first meeting. This kind of thinking says that if you're lucky, you might eventually develop a meaningful relationship with the guy you slept with the night before.

What a contrast to what God intends sex to be about. Some of the most beautiful language in the Bible, whether found in the story of creation or the Song of Solomon, was written about the marital relationship. When Bizzie and Brandon came before the altar of God, it was as two individual adults, children of the covenant and the pride of their parents. Yet, as we are told in Scripture, two shall become one. The vows they made that day gave words to this covenant, but sexual intercourse was the physical manifestation of the unity and oneness that had been achieved through the hard work of building a relationship.

Desperately Seeking…Intimacy

When you're young, your hormones seem to have more influence over you than anything else. But as you mature, a yearning that has always been a part of you takes root. Intimacy—oneness—is what we seek, and it doesn't evolve from sex. Instead, great sex evolves from an intimate relationship.

Stop for a minute and think about this. Introduction, friendship, courtship, engagement, marriage: the process of two separate human beings becoming one. This process is quite mysterious and not easily understood. Volumes have been written about it. Scientists and sociologists have studied it and songs have been composed about it. Ideally, the progression goes something like this:

1. Meet
2. Friendship
3. Love
4. Commitment
5. Engagement
6. Intimacy
7. Sex

Imagine instead that you meet at a party, recognize a spark between you, go to his place, and have sex for a while. He takes you home and may or may not call again, often on the basis of how good he thought the sex was. The progression is much simpler, and the outcome is very predictable:

1. Meet
2. Sex
3. Emptiness

Which of these progressions represents a truly happy couple enjoying a fulfilling sexual experience? Some women will argue that, in the second example, at least they had a pleasurable experience. Perhaps so, if you consider a fleeting burst of physical passion what you are looking for in life. In the introduction, I made it clear whom the intended audience for this book was. If you are satisfied with "At least I had a moment's pleasure," this book is not for you.

God didn't give us the instruction of no sex outside of marriage because He is mean and wants to take all of the fun out of life. He wants us to really enjoy sex and He knows the elements that are required to make that possible. If you are willing to do the hard work of building and maintaining a complex, intimate, and committed relationship, you will be rewarded with something that many women seek but too few find. You can be satisfied at the deepest level of emotional and spiritual need and have a passionate sex life that surpasses anything Hollywood could portray.

Intimacy is the sum of this book and so much more. It is the way your husband knows your body and your mind and your spirit. It is your willingness to be naked and vulnerable before him. It is the loving way his eyes smile at you in the morning and the soft way he whispers in your ear in the evening. "Place me like a seal over your heart..." says the beloved in the Song of Solomon, "for love is as strong as death, its jealousy unyielding as the grave. It burns like a blazing fire, like a mighty flame. Many waters cannot quench love; rivers cannot wash it away" (Song of Songs 8:6–7).

I've watched a couple of episodes of HBO's popular series, *Sex and the City*. Once you get past the filthy language, heavy drinking, and wanton promiscuity, it is almost surreal to imagine just what it is that these women are seeking. At the end of each episode, I felt only sympathy and sadness for these women, certainly no envy. The women go from sexual encounter to sexual encounter, purportedly looking for Mr. Right. Without even considering the potential for disease, crime, and physical abuse, they confuse sex with love, intercourse with intimacy, and contraception with commitment.

The good news is that though they don't get it, we can. Notwithstanding the image HBO is trying to convey, numerous studies indicate that married women are among the most sexually satisfied. A University of Chicago study found that "unmarried women are one and a half times more likely to have trouble climaxing than their married counterparts."[1] Forget the bar scenes portrayed on television. The people who have the most sex and are the happiest with their sex lives are monogamous couples. On the male side of things, married men are far less likely to report a lack of desire or erection problem than unmarried men.[2]

Intimacy between a man and a woman is what separates good from great. So if you don't feel satisfied in your own marital relationship, it may not be because of the nature, style, or frequency of your sex life; it may be that you and your husband have not achieved or aren't maintaining the intimacy you both need.

Finding Intimacy

If intimacy is the key, you probably are wondering how you can be assured it exists in your marital relationship. It develops over time, but only if a relationship includes honesty, openness, and vulnerability, both emotionally and physically.

Though there are no easy steps to achieve this, I believe that couples can do certain things that will help them develop an intimate relationship.

Define it.

First define what you mean by intimacy. Since intimacy is, by its nature, private and unique to your relationship, it will take some discussion for you to understand the concept of intimacy. It might go something like this at first: "Honey, I think we need to be more intimate." His initial response will likely be to think, *What in the world is she talking about?*

How do you articulate the concept? To him, intimacy will mean more sex. So you have to find the words to communicate this feeling of closeness and honesty, a sense of safety, trust, and security, a willingness to be vulnerable and open emotionally, physically, sexually, and spiritually. Both of you should be committed to trying to achieve this state of being. But it may take a while just to understand it.

Set it as a goal.

You have lists of goals and priorities for work, savings, weight loss, and so on. Don't just put intimacy away on a shelf and hope that you'll get to it one day. It should be the most significant part of your relationship, and working toward it should always be in the forefront of your relationship together.

Create a climate for intimacy to develop. When we plant seeds and want them to grow strong and healthy, we often put them in a hothouse where the conditions of moisture, temperature, and light are exactly right. We should bring this kind of thinking to our relationship as well and try to achieve conditions that are perfect for growing intimacy. Together, you and your husband should outline the changes you need to make in your lives together that will help intimacy to grow.

I have one important suggestion. I've heard a number of women state that if they don't feel loved, they cannot make love. We've let courtesy, civility, and kindness become small and unimportant parts of our relationships, and that has had a significant impact on our ability to be intimate. The prevailing thought among many is that chivalry is dead. We don't even bother to teach our children the basic rules of common courtesy.

When Charles stands and pulls out my chair as I return to our table in a restaurant, my heart soars. If he holds my coat and helps me as I struggle to find the sleeve or stands back and allows me to exit the elevator first, he communicates concern and care. This breeds an environment between us that is nurturing, secure, and loving: in other words, an environment conducive to intimacy and great sex. And just as courtesy and kindness are so effective at building this environment, so also do disrespect, incivility, and meanness quickly create the opposite atmosphere.

Work hard at it.

Once you have defined intimacy and set it as a goal, let the work begin. Just as the gardener will water and care for those seedlings every day, so too must we care for our budding intimacy.

If you were having trouble with your car or computer and couldn't fix it yourself, you would take it to a professional for assistance. Well, relationships are not much different, just a lot more important. If you are having real problems or difficulties, seek help and guidance. Some people bring real pathologies to their relationships, making it difficult at best and sometimes even impossible to break past barriers that took years to develop. We may need help in achieving intimacy with the people we love. Use mentors, if possible, or professional counselors. Building an intimate relationship that provides a sense of security, strength, trust, and commitment is the key to a long-lasting and fulfilling marriage—and a truly fabulous sex life.

Passion Killers

Whatever you do, don't underestimate the importance of achieving and maintaining intimacy in marriage, the most important of human relationships. Once you're working on that, you can move on to identifying the "passion killers" in your relationship.

Exhaustion.

In talking about sex and the "things I wish I had known," many women have told me that it was not so much what *they* wished they had known about sex when they got married as what they wished *their husbands* had known. The failure to appreciate a woman's exhaustion after a long day and its impact on her interest in sex seems to be the number one complaint I hear from women. So much turmoil in marriage seems to stem from this, rather than any specific missing element.

Men just don't expect exhaustion or depression or stress to be an impediment to sex. Instead they think, *She isn't interested in me. She doesn't love me. She doesn't like sex. She doesn't find me attractive. She doesn't want to have sex every day.*

Sadly, this can sometimes become a big crack in the marital relationship, particularly during the child-bearing and early childhood years. I remember going days and weeks feeling absolutely exhausted and incapable of any adult interaction, much less sex! However, if left untreated or unaddressed, it can create a big rift in a marriage. Once the pulling away happens, sometimes it takes intervention to pull back together. She can get angry and perceive that he is insensitive. She thinks that all he wants is sex, and he starts to think she is frigid. She has to be rested and ready; he is always ready, rested or not. Obviously you can see how quickly this could become a big issue.

Stress.

Emotionally, for most women to enjoy great sex, there has to be a stress-free environment, or at least an ordered, low-stress environment. For men, however, sex is often the first step to relieving stress. Imagine a high-powered attorney who hopes to make partner right before a major case. She was up late the evening before, studying her arguments and thinking through the questions she will ask the witnesses. As she lies in bed after a sleepless night, her mind struggles to focus. She has about two hours before she is due in court. She is stressed out to the max.

Meanwhile, on the other side of the bed, he's thinking, *Why not now? It will help her relax and get ready.* When she woke up that morning, sex was the last thing on her mind, though perhaps the first on his mind.

Flannel.

My favorite passion killer is flannel pajamas. I often have women come up to me and tell me that there is no romance, no spark in their bedroom. I ask them a few questions, one of which concerns what they wear to bed. I cannot tell you how many of them wear old, worn-out flannel pajamas. No wonder there is no excitement! Their husbands are probably having flashbacks to sleepovers at Grandma's—certainly not romantic thoughts!

Now, I use flannel as a symbol of an attitude that many women seem to have developed. Whether intentionally or not, it says, "Stay away, I'm not interested." For several years, Focus on the Family sponsored one-day conferences for women around the country entitled Renewing the Heart. I participated in these conferences and the portion of my talk about sex garnered the most responses, though it constituted only about five minutes of a forty-five-minute speech. All too often I heard from women who described sex in a passive way. This is terribly wrong and not what God intended.

We have a big role to play here! The first thing you can do is enjoy it—don't just lie there and let it happen to you. Be a participant—tell him what you want and what makes you feel good. Try new things in new places and at different times.

One of the things that troubled me when I talked to some of these women was that it seemed as if they were not trying in any way. They certainly weren't working on romance or trying to make themselves look beautiful in the eyes of their husbands. I guessed that if I went into their bedrooms and looked in their pajama drawers, I would find old flannel nightgowns and pajamas. Not the stuff of romance!

Out with the Passion Killers, In with the…

The first year I was with these women I gave them a homework assignment. (Lest you think I was trying to be like Dr. Ruth, let me add that they also got homework in health care, public policy, and spirituality.) I told each of them to stop at a Victoria's Secret or a similar store, preferably on the way home from the conference, and stock up on some intimate wear. If they could afford it, I recommended that they buy some lingerie in four different colors, definitely to include red! Then, to go home and seduce their husbands.

As I said, these were only five minutes of comments, so I didn't expect much of a response. But shortly thereafter, I started getting letters and e-mails detailing how these women had completed their homework. Most letters were giddy and inspiring—apparently all it took was a little push and being given the go-ahead for these women to reinvigorate their sex lives.

I remember one letter that included two large photographs. The first was a picture of several men holding up a banner that read, "Thank you, Kay." I thought it a little odd, until I saw the second picture—their wives, holding up the new lingerie that they had purchased, all with smiles on their faces.

By the time the second year rolled around, I started getting a few letters from women who said they had followed my directions, but nothing happened. One sister came up to my booth and said, "I did exactly what you told us the last time. I stopped in Victoria's Secret and went home and still couldn't interest my husband." I looked at her and I thought, *I don't know how to tell her!*

You see, that year we were talking about Esther and what she signified for women. Esther was a deep woman, and we can learn a lot from her. Scripture tells us that she was a very beautiful woman. Now that doesn't mean we should be intimidated by her because I sincerely believe that in Christ, all of us have the opportunity to be beautiful women.

But it does take a little bit more than just Victoria's Secret. You have to also stop at the cosmetics counter and at Bath & Body Works! As it says in Esther, "The girl pleased him and won his favor. Immediately he provided her with her beauty treatments and special food" (Esther 2:9). Now I'm not claiming that Esther was on the Atkins Diet or anything, but it does say she was on special foods. It said she had to complete twelve months of beauty treatments prescribed for the women, and she had six months of Oil of Olay and six with perfumes and cosmetics. So if I had anything to add to my previous homework assignment for the woman with the dispassionate husband, it is that she take the time to spiff up more than her lingerie selection.

Now, like Esther, I believe there should be no cover-up or false advertising. What we are talking about here are changes that will enhance our natural beauty. If you're like me, you can't take off a year and set it aside for just that purpose. So if you can't take a year, how about a day at the spa? Anybody can do that. If you can't afford a day at the spa, what about fifty dollars to fix up your bathroom and treat yourself to Oil of Myrrh, Oil of Olay, and Bath & Body Works?

If you can't afford that, just ask for something for your next birthday, anniversary, or Christmas. Each of us has inner beauty *and* physical beauty we can work at and enhance. It might mean dieting or exercising or improving our wardrobe. Whatever the case, it is a good thing to make yourself beautiful to your spouse.

Now I say this with a note of caution: Work on your body, but don't get all hung up on it. You're probably married to someone with his own set of issues: baldness, weight, wardrobe, and so on. Society has unfairly created a ninety-pound model as the epitome of womanhood. That is not what we are called to be.

What can be done about the passion killers? Sometimes, nothing at all or very little. We can't always control stress and exhaustion. We can minimize the impact they have on our relationship by getting rest and removing stress, but the bottom line is that sometimes you and your husband will have to recognize these things for what they are and deal with them on a daily basis. Don't panic or become overly concerned. There are many little things that you can do to help yourself relax and get in the mood: Treat yourself to a trip to the bookstore, a day at the spa, a getaway weekend, or a spiritual retreat. As we peel away the stress and the exhaustion—and perhaps the flannel nighties—it becomes a lot easier to rekindle the flames of passion.

Now, Let's Have Fun!

Though our culture seems to have deviated from the way God intended us to enjoy sex, it has always been a gift. We should not be embarrassed or hesitant to talk about pleasure in terms of the marriage covenant. When "properly executed" (define your own terms here), sex in an intimate, covenant relationship feels good and is fun and fulfilling. It is special to "know" one man and to know him really well. It is a way in which we express our commitment and the depth of our love for each other.

There is much to be learned from some of the writers and thinkers who approach these subjects from a secular perspective. Read them and then screen them through your own experience and theological persuasion. I have found much of Dr. John Gray's work (the bestselling author of *Men Are from Mars, Women Are from Venus*) to be entertaining and, although not "the" answer, somewhat helpful in understanding some principles of relationships. In his book *Mars and Venus in the Bedroom,* he introduced the different types of sex as they relate to mealtimes: fast food, home cooking, and gourmet meals. Since reading that together and talking and laughing with friends, Charles and I have added snacks and picnics. Can you see where this is going?

When I first got married, I thought that the formula for great sex was a romantic evening followed by passionate lovemaking. That's it. Each and every time, that's how it was supposed to happen. I thought that "anniversary" sex or "gourmet" sex was the norm: flowers, music, candles, beautiful lingerie, maybe even a little poetry thrown in. But who can live at that level constantly—and who wants to?

Home cooking is the standard. This kind of sex is warm, nurturing, comfortable, and quite satisfying when it is prepared with love! There are a lot of men and women out there who earnestly desire a good, home-cooked meal.

In a hurry? Don't have a lot of time? You still have to eat. Too tired and stressed out to cook? Fast food is the answer. You shouldn't maintain a steady diet of this, but it sure can meet a need and keep you from going hungry! Or how about a snack—something nutritious to hold you over until you can eat a full meal later?

And a picnic? Same food, different location can truly enhance the enjoyment of the meal.

Don't Forget the Details

Many women gave me small but important details concerning things they wish they had known about sex when they got married. Some were funny, some interesting, and some sad. Though this chapter is about the "big" parts of our relationships, these details bear mentioning.

- "Nobody, and I mean *nobody,* told me about the mess!" Keep little hand towels in the nightstand.
- "It took me years to relax and try new things. I wish that I had been more adventurous earlier. Wow!"
- "It's important to him that I initiate sex sometimes." If you haven't done this recently, make it a homework assignment to be completed in the next three days.
- "The Rollover Factor": When he rolls over and starts to snore, don't take it personally. To many men, sex is the ultimate sleeping pill. If it just got you started, though, refer to the previous suggestion.
- "Sex that hurts is *not* normal." Go to the doctor's office. It could be a bladder infection or other illness that is easily treatable.
- "Contraception is not always easy."
- "I didn't have to just lie there and pray for it to be over." Tell him what you like, what feels good and what doesn't.
- "Don't be afraid to laugh." When two people become contortionists, there is no telling what might happen. You're there to have fun, so laugh a little.

- "Buy a lock for your bedroom door and teach your kids to knock!"
- "I wish I had read a how-to book." The assumption in many marriage-preparation courses is that everyone either knows how to have great sex or learns quickly. A little guidance early in a marriage could improve things enormously. One of the most influential and helpful books for Christians is *Intended for Pleasure* by Ed and Gaye Wheat. In its third edition, this book has provided couples with a biblically and medically based reference book on sex.

Vive la Différence

When all is said and done, one of the most important things we can consider is how differently men and women view sex. And thank goodness for this! It's not a bad thing; it's just something we need to keep in mind. Sex is more important to men than it is to women. Intimacy is more important to women than it is to men. Just acknowledging this means that we are more likely to achieve what each of us wants.

Ten

Coping with Abuse

He couldn't have been a nicer guy when they got married. Sure, he had had some problems before that, but he had everything under control when the big day arrived. Now, after eight years of marriage, they had three wonderful children, a big house in the suburbs, and a good church, where he served as a deacon.

It wasn't until he lost his job that he started drinking again. He had stopped drinking when he became a Christian a couple of years before they were married. She thought that maybe the stress and frustration he was feeling made it easier to start again. At first it was just one drink or so at night. But then, as the days without work turned into weeks, he started to go out with his old friends again.

He still managed to clean up on Sunday mornings and was there at church, setting up chairs and handing out programs. No one suspected what was going on, and she didn't think it would help for her to be disloyal and talk about it. Instead she covered for him, even when he started getting abusive.

She never believed that he would hurt her. Sure, he got mean after a few drinks, but the kids were usually in bed by then, and she could handle the verbal abuse. She knew it was the alcohol talking, that she had married him for better or for worse. This would all pass when he got a job.

But it didn't. Even after he got a new job in the next town, he continued his drinking. She continued to cover for him with their family and friends, often telling them that he was sick—something she genuinely believed. The first time he hit her, she was really shaken. He didn't hurt her too much, but she had never believed him capable of that. After a couple of other times she began to get a little more defensive. She slept in the guest bedroom with the door locked when he went out. She started watering down the liquor, but he just drank more.

She couldn't leave him; she couldn't bear the thought of moving back to her parents' house with the children. And she had long ago let her cosmetology license lapse, so her skills were outdated. She felt she had no options. What would she do with the kids? How could she handle the shame?

Abuse Is a Many-Faceted Problem

Abuse is one of the most common reasons for serious marital problems and divorce. It can take on many forms—spiritual, emotional, physical—and it can stem from an addiction to drugs, alcohol, gambling, or pornography. Though each is different and has its own nuances, the patterns of abuse, denial, and destructive behavior can be the same regardless of the type. Good people from all walks of life spend all they have for one last roll of the dice, one last drink, one last fling with a joint. Whatever the form, the impact of this behavior is always devastating to a family.

If you are suffering some form of abuse in your marriage, you are not alone. You may think that you are the only one to whom this is happening, but the fact is that there are thousands of families—yes, even Christian families—going through the same things you are. There are thousands of women suffering from the same feelings of frustration, fear, and isolation.

Sadly, the facts testify to the widespread nature of abuse. According to the Bureau of Justice Statistics, there were 876,340 crimes committed by intimate partners against women in the United States. This included more than 1,300 murders of women by their partners.[1] The Department of Justice uses the term "intimate partners" to describe current or former spouses, boyfriends, or girlfriends. These crimes occur across all racial, ethnic, economic, and regional boundaries. We have witnessed a slight decline over the past decade, but the numbers are an obvious indicator that violence is still far too prevalent.

There are no statistics about abuse among Christians, but it is clear from the widespread abuse reported in every geographic, economic, and racial category that we are not immune to this. Remember: If you are suffering, it is not your fault, nor is it some aberration. Get some help.

A Suddenly Widespread Evil: Pornography

We often hear that alcohol and drugs are the most common forms of abuse in our society today. Fortunately, because of the widespread nature of this abuse, there are treatment programs and other means of support in virtually every community. Addiction is a powerful physical and psychological force, not only for the person suffering from it, but also for those around him or her. All too often physical abuse follows addiction, though in some cases it can also be the only form of abuse present in a relationship.

One of the most troubling forms of abuse in society today is addiction to pornography. You may not have noticed it, but the past decade has witnessed a revolution in pornography. No longer is it a seedy industry outside the mainstream, where dirty old men travel into bad neighborhoods to go to the adult bookstore or peep show. Pornographic magazines are sold in mainstream bookstores and convenience stores, "gentlemen's clubs" exist in many cities and towns, and pornographic video stars have become pop icons. And movies and music videos now feature a level of sexuality and nudity that would have been quickly banned less than ten years ago.

I have been amazed at the number of Christian women who have privately or publicly admitted that their husbands were "using" pornography. Gone is the shame that used to be associated with this. Gone, too, are the screams of oppression from national women's organizations. Some women have told me that their husbands have encouraged them to watch porn movies with them. I know that I'm old-fashioned, but sex is supposed to be private! (Unless, of course, you write an advice book and have an entire chapter on the subject!)

The Internet has had a hand in this. Though it has been responsible for wonderful changes in society—we can get more information than ever before, stay connected to distant friends and family, and save money when we make purchases—it has also enabled people to engage in very dangerous behavior. It has made every form of pornography, from pinups to bestiality and pedophilia, easily accessible from our homes. It has made the home computer a bookie's office. It enables a spouse and children to be involved in inappropriate, and sometimes illegal, relationships. Oftentimes it can hurt a marriage by drawing a person away from his or her spouse and family for extended periods of time. Chat rooms and cybersex are dangerous tools for marital estrangement.

Even innocent activity on the Internet can yield some unwanted responses. The Internet is not just words and pictures—

there's a lot of ugly substance behind this. If you conduct a word search, you are likely to get some sites that involve pornography or other dangerous information. Log on to any number of seemingly innocent Web sites and you will be instantly exposed to hard-core pornography. For a long time, the Clinton White House waged a legal battle with a pornography site that was using www.whitehouse.org to connect people to their site, when users were actually seeking the www.whitehouse.gov site.

You can wander into one of the many chat rooms on the Internet and be besieged by bizarre and disgusting offers. Those who are involved in counseling people with addictions or problems with pornography will tell you that the problem often starts with just a few pictures or a story, but it grows into a serious problem very quickly. The progressive nature of pornography addiction has destroyed many relationships. Good screening devices are available, which are great not only for your children, but also to protect adults from inadvertently becoming entangled in some of these sites.

Help is available, though not as widespread as Alcoholics Anonymous and other twelve-step programs. A good place to start on the Internet is with an organization called Christians in Recovery (www.christians-in-recovery.com), which not only offers some specific steps you can take but also links to organizations and help in your own community. Some sites and organizations are therapist based, as is SexualWholeness.com, which can be found at www.sexualwholeness.com.

There are other forms of abuse in marriage, including infidelity, verbal abuse, and workaholism. In some marriages, behavior that is inappropriate but not necessarily sinful becomes abusive. For example, it is inappropriate for a man to spend too much time with a woman who is not his wife. It becomes abusive when this relationship begins to harm the marriage by taking him away from his wife and placing the friend in an unsuitable role.

Whether it is an addiction to pornography, drugs, alcohol, or physical abuse, you are not powerless to fight it.

What You Can Do

Just because the abuse is occurring doesn't mean you can't do anything about it. You *must* do something about it—for yourself, your husband, your marriage, and your children. We are blessed to have access to a number of truly inspiring stories about women who have overcome some real adversity. A number of ministries, including Focus on the Family and the Christian Broadcasting Network, have books and pamphlets that tell some of these stories. I would encourage you to read some of these, regardless of your situation. (See the resource section for contact information.) In my own life, I have always been inspired by some of the slave stories and what women had to overcome to ensure their family's survival.

When we learn from these and other stories that our situations are not unique, we can find some definitive actions that work. Below you will find five steps that should be part of any woman's journey away from abuse.

1. Take control.

The first thing you must do is realize that you are not a helpless victim. You can let abuse control you or you can take control of the situation. I have a friend whom I admire a great deal for her strength and determination. Her husband had been involved repeatedly in poor business deals and bad investments that finally brought their family to financial ruin. They lost their house and cars, and they had to sell antiques they had inherited from her parents to make ends meet. They were past the limit on borrowing, and she couldn't seem to make him understand the situation. He always had one more scheme that would pull them out. A regular nine-to-five job was out of the question. After all, he pointed out, it wouldn't pay him what he thought he was worth, wouldn't use all of his talents, and working a desk job was just too confining. If she believed in him, she should quit nagging and have more patience. Everything would be all right.

Being without a phone for two weeks was bad enough, but when she picked up the kids from school and returned home to find the house cold and dark because the power had been turned off, she knew that she had to do something. She would get a job, get their lives organized, and give her husband an ultimatum. She knew that it wouldn't be easy, but it was their only chance.

She gathered her children around the kitchen table. She explained the situation to them and the decisions she had made. They prayed. They cried. Then they got up, determined to make it. (And they did!) That night she decided to stop being a victim and became a survivor. Up until that point, it was easy for her to be the one to whom things happened, so her real challenge now was to be the one who made things happen. In a way, it was all about whether she was going to eat dust or make dust.

She canceled all of their credit cards, took the kids and moved in with her parents, went out and found a job, and gave her husband an ultimatum to get his own life in order. I'm pleased to share with you that five years later and after much counseling and a renewed commitment, they are back together: happier, stronger, and wiser than ever before.

2. Use your options.

You must realize that you have options in your life. They are not always great ones, but the options are there. I am distraught every time I hear a woman say, "There's nothing I can do. I don't have any choice." That's like waving a white flag of surrender.

A woman recently shared her struggle with her husband's addiction to alcohol and drugs. Despite his abuse, manipulation, lying, and cheating, she stood by him. She tried to get him help. She tried several separations. She tried interventions. Nothing worked, but she stayed in this abusive relationship. Why? Because she never believed she had any other option. It wasn't just that she didn't believe in divorce; she didn't really believe in herself either. Finally, years later, she realized that she was willing to do anything but stay any longer and be abused.

We always have options. Many women can't see them or aren't willing to exercise them until they're desperate. Sometimes we just need help identifying them. This is where a mentor, a good pastor, a sister-girlfriend, or a "mother of the church" can be especially helpful.

3. Don't hide it.

Why are we such enablers? Is it to avoid shame? Protect our reputation? Is it because of pride or because we don't want to admit failure? As was the case in the anecdote at the beginning of this chapter, many women hide the abuse that goes on in their marriages out of embarrassment, shame, or guilt. Unfortunately, this enables even more of the negative behavior. It doesn't do either of you any good to cover abuse. As Christians we are called to shine the light on sin and to stand for righteousness.

We create, or perpetuate, a crisis by hiding the problem until it's too late. Many situations are easier to deal with if they are confronted early in the process. It is emotionally good for you to share your burden. In fact, it is the first step of the healing process. As Paul wrote in Galatians 6:2, "Carry each other's burdens, and in this way you will fulfill the law of Christ."

One note of caution: You must not hide abuse, but be careful with whom you share the information. Make certain that it is someone who can help you.

4. Get help.

Whatever your situation, there is a great deal of help available to you: pastoral care from church, psychotherapy, physical protection. If nothing else, start with self-help literature and groups, such as Alcoholics Anonymous, Narcotics Anonymous, My Sister's Keeper (a Christian group offering assistance for any form of violence against women; call toll-free: 1-888-988-0988), and many others, including local shelters and help lines.

I say this with some caution. Too many people try to solve a problem themselves, partly because they do not want to admit it to others. You cannot treat abuse with a diet plan or a new technique of money management. Don't fool yourself into thinking that you can fix an abusive situation alone. While it might be acceptable to start slowly, sometimes you can resolve a problem much more quickly if you seek direction from an expert.

Unfortunately, many Christians avoid seeking qualified and competent help. Part of this is because there have been a number of instances in which modern psychology is used to subtly belittle Christian beliefs and values. For instance, a secular therapist working with a Christian suffering from depression may encourage the exploration of behaviors that are against the client's principles. Unfortunately, this has led many devout Christians to conclude that mainstream psychology has no place in the healing of their emotional difficulties.

The truth is that psychology is nothing more than the science of human behavior, and Christians have nothing to fear from research-based findings. For example, research shows that major depression can be treated effectively with a combination of cognitive psychotherapy—which addresses negative thought patterns—and antidepressants (if needed). It is not anti-Christian to seek professional help to overcome a major depression any more than it is to seek professional help for ulcers. However, the psychologist or psychiatrist chosen should be able to demonstrate that he is both competent and sensitive to his clients' beliefs and values. For best results, get a recommendation from a friend who has had success with a particular counselor or a local ministry that specializes in your needs.

Be aware that church leaders are not necessarily the most appropriate source of counsel when you are dealing with serious emotional problems. A sensitive church leader should be able to recognize the difference between personal/spiritual growth issues and serious mental disorders. For instance, a parishioner struggling to overcome a particular sin or problem in living can be well served by pastoral or lay counseling. But a member experiencing a clinical depression needs professional help and needs it quickly. If someone suggests that your long-lasting depression is a symptom of weak faith, look elsewhere for aid.

There is no shame in the eyes of God for a Christian to seek help and to find healing through the tools of psychology. On the other hand, there is much needless harm when churches discourage people from getting professional help for emotional difficulties. Such churches add to the already great burden of a soul in need.

5. Get out.

Sometimes the only thing left to do is get out of the abusive situation. You have to decide what's best for you, your husband, and your children and take steps to protect each of you. This doesn't necessarily mean you must get out of the marriage, though it might be appropriate in some cases. You will recall that we talked about the role of separation in marriage. In many instances, separation is an appropriate and immediate step. Sometimes it helps the husband to hit rock bottom and begin the difficult road to recovery. Sometimes all it does is get you out of the line of fire.

I have found Dr. Dobson's book on this subject *Tough Love* to be quite compelling. The pain of being involved with someone engaged in self-destructive behavior is horrible, but the solution cannot be your own destruction and that of your children. Some couples say that they stay together "for the children's sake." Very often, this does more harm than the abuse itself. In the case of physical abuse, it teaches your daughters that it is acceptable to take abuse from a man and your sons that it is acceptable to abuse a woman. By removing yourself and the children, you not only save your family, but you also demonstrate to your children what is and is not acceptable behavior.

Know that God's help is near. The psalmist wrote that the Lord God "heals the brokenhearted and binds up their wounds" (Psalm 147:3). Sadly, we still have far too much abuse, even in Christian homes. This is not a normal part of marriage, nor is it a reflection of your failure. I am not an expert in any of the pathologies that engender abuse, but I can give you rock-solid advice: If you are in an abusive situation, please seek professional assistance. Don't delay.

Eleven

Crisis Points

There is, in every woman's heart, a spark of heavenly fire, which lies dormant in the broad daylight of prosperity, but which kindles up and beams and blazes in the dark hour of adversity.

WASHINGTON IRVING

My grandmother used to say, "All you have to do, girl, is live long enough and trouble will come knocking on your door." She was by no means a pessimistic person, and she never meant this to be a statement of surrender. Rather, she was a woman old enough and wise enough to know that every person's life involves great happiness and joy, *as well as* crises, difficulty, and pain. We all seem to be raised to take the high points of life—the births, graduations, loves, marriages—for granted and to expect that they will be part of our lives. Rarely do we consider that the low points are as important and as predictable a part of life as well.

In the preceding chapters, we have talked about some tough times and circumstances that occur in many marriages. I think it is helpful to try to discern what constitutes a real crisis and what is simply a difficult situation or a disappointment. It's easy when we are disappointed or frustrated or unhappy to assume that we are in the midst of a crisis. But you can't be a gutsy, sophisticated millennium woman and go into a major meltdown because your child didn't get into the "right" kindergarten.

A crisis has eternal consequences or is something that strikes deeply at one's core values and principles. The American Heritage Dictionary defines a crisis as "an emotionally stressful event or a traumatic change in a person's life."[1] We sometimes need to step back and get some perspective on this, perhaps try to see things from God's perspective and understand His purpose.

A couple of years ago, while on a trip, I received a call from my niece Rita. She was living with us while attending law school, and she wanted to prepare me for what awaited me on my return. She knew and loved her aunt Kay, and she understood and loved her younger cousins as well. She wanted to give Charles and me time to process the fact that Robbie had come home from college sporting a diamond stud in his ear. (By the way, it wasn't a real diamond. He may have been crazy enough to get his ear pierced, but he wasn't crazy enough to spend what little money he had on a real stone!) He would be home by the time we got in from a four-hour trip back from Washington, D.C. My response? First anger, then hurt, then tears—and then I repeated the entire cycle again. Charles was determined to rip out the earring and be done with the problem—end of discussion. (Life is so simple for men sometimes!)

By the time we got home all I could do was look at my baby, cry, then crawl into bed to escape reality by watching an old black-and-white movie. You know the kind: Boy meets girl, boy does something stupid, couple finally gets together and struggles through some problems, and then everything works out with a backdrop of snow and Bing Crosby's crooning.

Charles took Robbie for a ride and they talked. The compromise was that he would not wear the earring in our presence. At the time, it just hurt me too much to see it.

In retrospect, the picture must have been pretty comical: curtains drawn, a darkened room, Lana Turner in black-and-white—and me in the fetal position under my blankets. After about three hours of this "crisis" (I had to finish the movie once I started it), I realized how pathetic I was. This was a pierced ear, not some catastrophe. Robbie was twenty-one and not my baby anymore. I needed to save the drama for important stuff: a moral crisis, a major illness, a death in the family.

Incidentally, after a few months we apologized to our twenty-one-year-old. We raised our kids to be independent thinkers. The fact that the earring caused me pain was not sufficient reason for me to ask him to change his personal style. We told him to be true to himself and that we would deal with our own emotions and issues. (By the way, we're seeing the earring less and less, so maybe one day…)

What We Can Control

A number of years ago a group of insurance companies conducted a study in the major crises in people's lives and weighted each crisis. Their purpose was to determine the impact and primary causes of severe stress and then use the findings to decide how to insure high-risk individuals. The types of things that constituted a significant crisis included death of a spouse, disability, death or serious illness of a child, divorce, death of a parent, job change or loss, and moving. You can imagine my surprise when I discovered that I qualified for the same life insurance premium as someone with congestive heart failure! We had just recently recovered from Bizzie's illness, the aunt who had raised me had died, and Charles was going through a job change and transfer. With four of the crises identified in this study occurring at once, it seemed like no part of our life was stable.

This study may have been revealing to the insurance industry, but I think we all know that life is a series of crises, both big and small, for each and every one of us. No one is exempt from this because of lifestyle, faith, or isolation. Nor is there much a person can do to prevent some crises from happening; in fact, many are beyond our control altogether. Often, as if in some extreme test of character, multiple crises occur at the same time or one right after another. (Remember Job?)

What we can control is how we respond to the crises in our lives, how we grow from each experience, and how we handle adversity as a family unit. We can learn patience and perseverance, how to be strong, and what it means to have trust and faith. Character is not the only thing to come out of a crisis; oftentimes, a deep and personal awareness of God's presence in our lives arises as well.

Crisis points are times when we *have* to trust God. We have to be able to first discern the real crises in our lives and then take steps to deal with them. Many people make the mistake of discounting the impact of crisis points upon a marriage (if not handled properly, a serious crisis can destroy a marriage). Even more people believe themselves helpless to respond. It's too easy to play the victim (even if we are) and ask, *Why me, God?* A more appropriate attitude might be: *Why not me? What makes me so special that I, above all others, should be exempt from life's crisis points? What can I do to get through this and maybe even grow a little in the process?*

Types of Crises

We've identified what a crisis is and acknowledged that you are likely to experience many in a lifetime. Perhaps one of the most comforting things about going through a crisis is the knowledge that you are not the first to do so. Whatever the crisis point—death, illness, divorce—millions of other people have gone through what you are going through, maybe even worse. This means that there are support groups, counselors, and Christian literature that can help you identify and cope with your situation.

I'm not going to attempt to list every possible crisis that will hit your marriage. For the purposes of our discussion, however, I will categorize them into three broad groups. These categories can and do overlap sometimes, and occasionally a crisis can move in and out of different categories.

Life crises.

In the first category are those crises which pertain to life itself. They include the death of a parent, spouse, or child; a miscarriage; or a severe illness or disability. The death of a loved one is always a crisis because it has eternal consequences and will affect you in many unforeseen ways. Despite the fact that it is a given part of life, we are rarely prepared for it and sometimes surprised by how it impacts other relationships.

The death of her mother was the first crisis that Rene and her husband, Jonathon, faced. It seemed that they had only just begun their life together when a drunk driver took her relatively young mother's life. In the first week or two, Rene was on autopilot. Jonathon's role seemed easy then: making funeral arrangements, talking to well-intentioned friends who called and visited, freezing all the food that got dropped off, and holding his sobbing wife tightly whenever she needed him.

After a couple of weeks, though, things got complicated. They both had to go back to work, which at first seemed helpful to Rene. But because her mother had died unexpectedly and been unprepared legally, it meant that Rene had to deal with banks and courts and realtors. Getting through that was difficult enough; she never expected her family to cause so many problems. Normally her brothers and sisters got along fine, but now it seemed that everyone wanted the same things from her mother's house, no one trusted the others, and everyone was mad all of the time.

You would think that the spouse of the person who lost a parent would easily fit into the role of supporter and encourager. But husbands and wives sometimes have difficulty trying to be supportive. Should you try to pick up his spirits or back away and give him time to grieve? Should you venture an opinion about how things should be disposed of or stay out of your husband's family business? What, for instance, is the role of the wife when her husband has to resolve issues with his brothers over his father's estate? Does she offer advice, voice her opinions, or just keep her mouth closed? The wrong decision can put a strain on your marriage. There is no one correct technique for helping a spouse in crisis, but these are issues you will likely have to face. When in coping/supporting mode, learn from others who have navigated tragedy and seek counsel from them.

Possibly the most traumatic experience for a family is the death of a child. Sadly, too many parents learn that there is no pain like the pain of a child's serious illness or death. Though we did not lose her, Bizzie's near-fatal illness as a four-year-old was the most difficult experience we ever faced as a family. The pain and fear were so intense that there were moments I was certain Charles and I could not survive. Likewise, the joy and happiness of her recovery have never left us and assure us that each day with our children is indeed special.

Those couples who have lost a child know a pain that we can

only pray we do not experience. The intensity of grief often dev-astates a family, and though many find strength and meaning in this experience, some families never recover without professional help. Without that help, the sadness, pain, blame, and loss may be too much to overcome.

Lifestyle traumas.

The second category of crisis contains those events or changes that I do not believe, based on my previous definition, are truly crises—meaning they do not have eternal consequences or affect core val-ues and principles. I recognize, however, that for many people, these are significant events that cause very real distress and pain. I call these the "lifestyle traumas"—changes that affect the manner in which we live. For most people, these are generally related to finan-cial crises, including job change or loss, and moving.

Possibly the best protection against these types of problems is having a "cushion." A cushion of regular, wise health habits can help you get through a bout with pneumonia. A cushion of financial resources can help you get through car repairs. A cush-ion of friends and family can help you survive the emotional trauma of being without a job when the plant closes.

Human crises.

The third category of crises involves the most complicated and difficult to address, in my opinion. I call them the "living" or "human" crises. These are the traumas that relate to our flawed nature as human beings and some of the painful things we do to one another as a result of poor choices. The so-called midlife cri-sis, which causes so much destruction in families today, is one example. These crises can be more complicated than those in the other categories. They are more difficult to identify and often are incidents you do not want to share with anyone. Think about the trauma that a moral failure by a spouse or child can cause.

Reconciliation, in these cases, can be difficult. Some believe that infidelity is the only cause of divorce permitted in the Bible. But there are other types of moral failure that couples sometimes face. Before deciding how to proceed, you must determine where you both are spiritually. If the offending spouse acknowledges his sin, repents for the harm he has caused, and desires reconciliation, that presents one path. If, however, the offending partner does not, then reconciliation may be more difficult or even impossible. Whatever the situation, counseling from a spiritual advisor, pastor, or mentor is critical to help you survive and overcome this crisis.

Surviving the Crisis Points

When my mother died, I was surprised by how much it hurt. I thought that because my theology was sound and I loved and trusted God and knew that she was with Him, it would somehow hurt less. It didn't. The pain was mental, emotional, and sometimes physical. There seemed to be no comfort.

Around that time, I was contacted by my friend Terri McFaddin. She is a gifted songwriter and author. Terri advised me to start listening, really listening, to music. When you can't read the words on paper because of the tears in your eyes, when your grief is so strong that you feel physical pain, she reminded me that music can minister to your spirit. Get a small tape player, she told me, and listen to whatever it is that touches your spirit. For me, it has always been black gospel. Since then, I have always turned to music when confronting a crisis. Kirk Franklin, Yolanda Adams, and the Brooklyn Tabernacle Choir have pulled me through on many occasions.

That's just one small coping mechanism. Everyone has something that works particularly well for her. We all know that the crisis points will happen to us, perhaps even today. There are some overall principles that I believe can help us survive when things go wrong.

Have a safe harbor.

Establish a place where you can go to weather the storm safely. For me, this means having a supporting and encouraging home environment—a place where I can feel the warmth and security of my family, comforted by the things I know. When I was the chairman of the gambling commission, the media used to beat me up in the news regularly. We had deadlines, research and personnel problems, a hectic travel schedule, and many issues to juggle. I organized my home knowing that I would need a place that was large enough for me to have everyone for Sunday dinner and small enough that I could feel pampered when it was just Charles and me.

Your home should be the safe and warm place in which you feel most comfortable during times of crises. It might just be a special room or perhaps a bedroom and bathroom that you have outfitted with things that will make you feel better. Whatever the place, just knowing that you have a safe refuge is the first step to getting through a difficult time.

This need not cost a lot of money. Warmth and security can be conveyed in many different ways, depending on your personality. Winding down is extremely difficult for me. I take my work home—the paperwork and the mental work. A day at the spa is out of the question (who has the time or money?). But a few purchases and I transformed my bathroom into a day spa. A few candles and my favorite compact disc and I'm halfway there!

Following Edith Schaeffer's advice, I can even transform a sterile hotel room into a safe haven with a few extra things from home thrown into my suitcase—some pictures, candles, a Bible, and other books. There are some months when I am on the road twenty out of thirty days and rarely for more than one night in the same city. Some women's groups to which I have spoken have been incredibly sensitive and put flowers, homemade treats, magazines, and other special gifts in my hotel room to make it more pleasant. I have always appreciated these warm and thoughtful touches.

Eliminate stress.

The second step is to eliminate any unnecessary stress factors in your life. If you have meetings that you regularly attend, drop them from your calendar for a while. They will survive and you could use the break. If you take care of an elderly aunt, ask another niece or nephew to do so for a while. If you can put your bills on automatic deduction so that you don't have to worry about the electric bill while you are sorting out a crisis, do it.

This is where having the cushion that I mentioned earlier is so helpful. The last thing you want to worry about during a crisis is money. Having a savings account for emergencies may alleviate some of the stress you are experiencing.

One of the best ways to eliminate unnecessary stress is the third step:

Take all the help you can get.

In trying to get through a crisis, it is essential that we remember that no one can do it alone. We are designed by God for fellowship with Him and each other. It is my faith alone that has brought me through some tough times. At other times, it was the support structure of friends and family that did it. This is where the work we discussed in the preventative care chapter comes in. I think every church should have an effective ministry organized to help families survive a crisis. This ministry should include the entire package of pastoral care—spiritual support, counseling, and practical help.

I know it can be hard to accept the generosity of others, particularly strangers. Oftentimes it is simply misplaced pride that causes us to decline offers of assistance. Sometimes we think that the person is offering help just to make the offer. Be gracious and accept what is offered out of love and concern. If you are on the other end, make genuine offers or find out from others what you can do to help. Likewise, if your church does not have a pastoral care program that provides assistance to families in need, this is a great ministry for you to help start. I sometimes think that we go through crises to learn to empathize with those in pain. We can use this knowledge wisely to enrich others' lives.

When I first became the Secretary of Health and Human Resources in Virginia, we had a long cold spell that forced us to focus a lot of attention of the plight of the homeless. I met with several groups involved in the care of these men, women, and children to help devise ways to protect them from the bitter cold and to get them into permanent housing. I think I shocked many of the advocates when I announced that I did not believe that we had a problem with homelessness in Virginia. After they all caught their breath, I explained that what I saw was a problem of disconnectedness.

When our daughter was ill, the deacons sent over a chart every week that told us how all of our practical needs would be met: who would baby-sit the boys, who was bringing dinner, which women in the church were going to clean the house, who would be praying for us. The young adults group even decorated the house for Christmas and put up a tree. Neither Charles nor I had the desire or the energy, but boy were we glad they had done it when the doctors allowed Bizzie to come home from the hospital for a few hours on Christmas Day. Without these supports, I'm not sure our family could have survived this ordeal.

You see, each of the homeless was someone's brother or sister or friend or neighbor. They were individuals who somehow became disconnected from the support structure that family, friends, churches, and neighborhoods provide them, faced a crisis or two, and ended up on the streets. Our response as a community should not be simply to find them shelter for the coldest nights, but to try to help them rebuild the connections that would prevent them from becoming homeless in the future.

I know, for instance, that whatever happens to me—whether I suffer from any emotional, psychological, or physical problem—that I will never have to spend one day going hungry. I have brothers, cousins, children, friends, and a church family, all of whom would make certain that I was cared for properly. Surviving hardship is all about community, a critical concept that seems to have been lost in our nation. And to those who are alone and disconnected, for whatever reason, we have a responsibility to respond with justice and mercy, in practice and in policy. I believe that should be part of our mission as a church and as individual Christians.

When I was in Richmond, I met a group of women from a local Baptist church who understood this concept. Anyone who knows me even slightly knows that I come out of that black Southern tradition that says that any crisis should be met head-on with a home-cooked meal. These women read a story in the newspaper that detailed a difficult job I had been asked to do and guessed what it would mean to me and my family. They rose to the occasion with a "ministry" of freezer meals. Even though I had no time to cook, Charles and I could unwind to the savory aroma of one of these freezer meals within thirty minutes of getting home. More important, we knew that we were loved and cared for by our community.

I know that many of my colleagues in the public arena have benefited from the prayers offered on their behalf when they face a difficult time. Whether it is someone preparing for a Senate confirmation hearing or working through a difficult issue, the "hedges of protection" that come through phone calls, personal visits, and e-mail make a tremendous difference.

If you're the friend or relative offering assistance, please know that there are no right words at times of crises. No matter how close you are, it's going to be difficult. But there is one wrong thing you can say, and it's only after going through a crisis that you understand it. Try not to say, "If you need anything, just let me know." Though it is generally said with the best of intentions, rarely do those in need ever respond. Instead, just offer or *just do* whatever you think might be helpful. Here in the South, we always send food—it seems we believe a ham and rolls can make any crisis seem easier!

Take the time to feel.

The fourth step is critical and one that many of us have tried to deny: actually feeling the appropriate emotions, whether they are grief, anger, remorse, or whatever. In the movie *Ordinary People,* the psychologist played by Judd Hirsch summed it up correctly: "The only way you can prevent feeling pain is to not feel anything." When I face a crisis, sometimes the most important thing I can do is to climb into bed, get into a fetal position, and work through my emotions. Some people try to prevent themselves from feeling these emotions and end up extending the crisis unnecessarily or creating another crisis.

It is also imperative that you know when to put these emotions aside, or at least let something else be felt. Grief, for instance, can consume you. If you try to deny it at the time, you will add guilt and other stress to your life. If you give in completely to the grief, you might never reclaim your life. You have to find a way to feel the grief and feel it completely for a while and then learn how to move it from the forefront of your emotions. Don't set big goals or try to make big changes—start with small steps. Time does indeed heal pain, though sometimes we simply have to learn to live with it.

Express your emotions.

Take the time not only to express your emotions in appropriate ways but also to express them to the appropriate people. Don't shut your husband out of what you are feeling; it's important to both of you to share what you are going through. If others are involved in the crisis, share your thoughts and feelings with them in a way that does not violate the trust and intimacy of your marital relationship.

Charles had me absolutely confused when Bizzie was sick. His method of coping was to deny that she was seriously ill and continue to get up, get dressed, and go off to work every day. In other words, he checked out. When he was standing by her bed and she had a cardiac and respiratory arrest, he could no longer deny what was going on. The flood of emotions came rushing forward after weeks of denial.

I needed to understand that everyone has different coping mechanisms. I had to back off and let him cope in the way that he knew how. And he needed to understand my need for him to be there physically and emotionally.

Take good care.

The sixth step is overlooked too often. In getting through a crisis point, you must take care of yourself and your family. I know of so many women who just let themselves fall apart when they face a crisis in their lives. You have to eat and rest and stay well if you are going to be able to weather the storm. If you already exercise, don't stop. The routine itself is as beneficial to weathering the crisis as is the impact of the exercise to your health. And sleep: It is amazing to me how important sleep is in getting through a difficult time. Sometimes just sleeping for a day or so can do more good than anything else.

Get perspective.

The seventh step is to try to put the crisis in perspective. When you are in the midst of trauma, sometimes the only thing that can truly help is time and knowing that God has a plan for all of this. I remember once feeling as if I were on one of those mechanical bulls that you see in western movies. All I wanted to do was stay on until the clock ran out. I didn't care how I looked or how I performed—I just wanted to stay on. Every time I thought I had weathered the bucking and twisting, it started again.

Many painful things get easier with time, but occasionally you have to take small steps before you can run again. I had a good friend who had a long and painful battle with breast cancer, and eventually died. Despite my faith and the knowledge that she was with God, the grief was consuming and took me out for the count. Finally I realized that I had to get up again, but I couldn't face the prospect of anything major at first. So I made a list of really minor, unimportant things (change the sheets, clean the bathroom, bake bread) that had to be done and began to check them off slowly. Within a day or two, I was engrossed in catching up.

That didn't mean I stopped grieving, merely that a little time went a long way. Take action, if it's needed. I've seen a bumper sticker that reads, "If you feel like you're going through hell, keep going!"

Pray.

Don't be afraid to ask God to help you through the crisis. We have an amazing ability to do some of our best praying when we are facing tough times. Your faith plays a critical role in your ability to survive a crisis. It is important that you trust God, particularly when things don't seem to make sense. Faith cannot shield you from pain, but it does help you as you walk through it.

Take a break.

Many grief counselors encourage people to go away for a few days, change the scenery, and start anew. Back when the kids were small and Charles and I were enduring a particularly stressful period, some friends at church gave us a "free" weekend. On Friday evening, someone picked up the kids and took them away for the weekend. That first evening alone was awkward, difficult, and stressful—would you believe it? Without the kids to direct the conversation, Charles and I just sat there and stared at each other. I remember going to bed thinking that it was going to be a huge waste of a weekend.

By Saturday, we thought we might as well take advantage of the time alone, and we did some things that we had wanted to do for several months but couldn't because of the kids. As the day progressed, we both found ourselves really having fun together and remembering how much we enjoyed each other's company. By Sunday, we were ready to pawn the children off to anyone who would take them for a few more days.

That weekend had an enormous impact on me. Not only did the memory bring me happiness, but the knowledge that the spark still existed between us reenergized me to deal with everyday life.

I know our relationship needs to be cared for and nurtured, but I am also aware that I am not alone on my journey. I have a partner who will walk alongside me through some of the most difficult crises, sometimes pushing and sometimes pulling, and will always be there. And that, after all, is the essence of marriage.

My grandmother was right: Trouble will always come knocking. But even if we have to answer the door, we don't have to face the crisis point on the other side alone. As you endure crises in your marriage, know that God stands with you to keep you strong and wise through all the pain. Know that thousands of women have likely gone through the same situation and survived. And every day is an opportunity to grow. Be encouraged!

Conclusion

L ast year a friend forwarded me an e-mail attachment entitled "How to Be a Good Wife," a section taken out of a
home-economics textbook from the 1950s. This unat-
tributed list has been widely circulated over the Internet, and
nothing I have seen better illustrates the difference between 1950
and today. It also provides a springboard for my final thoughts to
you.

In that bygone era, educators recommended the following to
teenage girls:

1. Have dinner ready: Plan ahead, even the night before, to
   have a delicious meal—on time. This is a way of letting
   him know that you have been thinking about him and are
   concerned about his needs. Most men are hungry when
   they come home, and the prospects of a good meal are
   part of the warm welcome needed.

2. Prepare yourself: Take fifteen minutes to rest so you will be
   refreshed when he arrives. Touch up your makeup, put a
   ribbon in your hair, and be fresh looking. He has just been
   with a lot of work-weary people. Be a little gay and a little
   more interesting. His boring day may need a lift.

3. Clear away the clutter: Make one last trip through the

main part of the house just before your husband arrives, gathering up schoolbooks, toys, paper, etc. Then run a dust cloth over the tables. Your husband will feel he has reached a haven of rest and order, and it will give you a lift, too.

4. Prepare the children: Take a few minutes to wash the children's hands and faces if they are small, comb their hair, and if necessary change their clothes. They are little treasures, and he would like to see them playing the part.

5. Minimize the noise: At the time of his arrival, eliminate all noise of washer, dryer, or vacuum. Encourage the children to be quiet. Be happy to see him. Greet him with a warm smile and be glad to see him.

6. Some don'ts: Don't greet him with problems or complaints. Don't complain if he's late for dinner. Count this as minor compared to what he might have gone through that day.

7. Make him comfortable: Have him lean back in a comfortable chair or suggest he lie down in the bedroom. Have a cool or warm drink ready for him. Arrange his pillow and offer to take off his shoes. Speak in a low, soft, soothing, and pleasant voice. Allow him to relax and unwind.

8. Listen to him: You may have a dozen things to tell him, but the moment of his arrival is not the time. Let him talk first.

9. Make the evening his: Never complain if he does not take you out to dinner or to other places of entertainment; instead, try to understand his world of strain and pressure, his need to be home and relax.

10. The goal: Try to make your home a place of peace and order where your husband can relax.

AUTHOR UNKNOWN

Fortunately, some sister decided that this list needed a bit of updating. This twenty-first-century version has also had a wide circulation on the Internet, though its original author is likewise not listed anywhere.

1. Have dinner ready: Make reservations ahead of time. If your day becomes too hectic, just leave him a voice-mail message regarding where you'd like to eat and at what time. This lets him know that your day has been crazy and gives him an opportunity to change your mood.

2. Prepare yourself: A quick stop at the Lancôme counter on your way home will do wonders for your outlook and will keep you from becoming irritated every time he opens his mouth. (Don't forget to take his credit card!)

3. Clear away the clutter: Call the housekeeper and tell her that any miscellaneous items left on the floor by the children can be placed in the Goodwill box in the garage.

4. Prepare the children: Send the children to their rooms to watch television or play video games.

5. Minimize the noise: If you happen to be home when he arrives, be in the bathroom with the door locked.

6. Some don'ts: Don't greet him with problems and complaints. Let him speak first, and then your complaints will get more attention and remain fresh in his mind throughout dinner. Don't complain if he's late for dinner, simply remind him that the leftovers are in the fridge and you left the dishes for him to do.

7. Make him comfortable: Tell him where he can find a blanket if he's cold. This will really show you care.

8. Listen to him—but don't ever let him get the last word.

9. Make the evening his: Never complain if he does not take

you out to dinner or other places of entertainment; go with a friend or go shopping (use his credit card). Familiarize him with the phrase "girls' night out."

10. The goal: Try to keep things amicable without reminding him that he only thinks the world revolves around him. Obviously he's wrong; it revolves around you.

Now, kidding aside, there really is a little truth in both. What the 1950s woman knew is that courtesy, kindness, thoughtfulness, and demonstrative love are important in a marriage. What her list doesn't convey is that this is a two-way street and that both husband and wife must do this consistently and intentionally. The twenty-first-century woman knows who she is. She knows that a little time spent on herself is a good thing. She knows that she is not there to be a doormat for her husband.

Perhaps that is the secret of the millennium wife—that she can combine the best of the past, be it 1950 or 2001, to have the strongest, most intimate, and most fulfilling marital relationship.

I have been blessed with extraordinary gifts and opportunities in my life. In addition to a loving and supportive husband and three remarkable children who love God, I have had jobs that have offered me the opportunity to serve our nation and, hopefully, impact our culture. As someone who came from public housing projects, born to a mother on welfare and an absentee father addicted to the debilitating effect of alcohol, I find the chance to sit across the table from the President of the United States and discuss public policy a testament to this great land of opportunity. Even more incredible to me, the chance to be a wife and mother in a stable, intact, two-parent, God-loving family is a testament to God's everpresent grace and redemption.

There is nothing wasted in your life: no hardship, no turmoil, no problem. Everything is something God can use to make you into the woman He needs you to be for kingdom work. Yes, there's a lot that I wish I had known earlier in my life and in my marriage. But you know, I don't think God ever lets us stop learning; He doesn't ever stop providing us with opportunities. In His kingdom, there are never any regrets. And you know of all the things I've learned over the years, I never learned anything one day too late. Neither will you.

Multnomah Publishers

The publisher and author would love to hear your comments about this book. *Please contact us at:* www.multnomah.net/keepinitreal

Resource Guide

Books

The books listed below are a few of the many that are available on the subjects addressed in this book. As I noted previously, some of the works by Edith Schaeffer, Jim Dobson, Gary Smalley, Ron Blue, and Larry Burkett were all instrumental in forming and sustaining my own marriage. Your relationship is a lifelong endeavor, so find the ones that are right for you and will help your marriage to grow.

General

Dobson, James. *Love for a Lifetime: Building a Marriage That Will Go the Distance.* Portland, Ore.: Multnomah, 1987. One of the most influential books written for couples with tips, stories, and an inspiring message.

——. *Love Must Be Tough/Straight Talk.* Nashville, Tenn.: Thomas Nelson, 1999.

——. *Romantic Love: Using Your Head in Matters of the Heart.* Ventura, Calif.: Regal Books, 2000.

——. *What Wives Wish Their Husbands Knew about Women.* Wheaton, Ill.: Tyndale, 1977.

——. *The Keys to a Lifelong Love.* Nashville, Tenn.: Word, 2000.

Field, David. *Marriage Personalities*. Eugene, Ore.: Harvest House, 1986. A helpful guide to determining the types and effects of the personalities involved in your marriage.

Mason, Mike. *The Mystery of Marriage: As Iron Sharpens Iron*. Portland, Ore.: Multnomah, 1985. An unusual but beautiful discussion of the marriage relationship from beginning to end.

Meredith, Don. *Becoming One: Planning a Lasting, Joyful Marriage*. Nashville, Tenn.: Thomas Nelson, 1979.

Meredith, Don and Sally. *Two...Becoming One: Experiencing the Power of Oneness in Your Marriage*. Chicago: Moody Press, 1999.

Schaeffer, Edith. *A Celebration of Marriage*. Grand Rapids, Mich.: Baker Books, 1994. Beautiful and common-sense insights into a remarkable marriage.

—. *What Is a Family?* Grand Rapids: Baker Books, 1975. The classic that explains the importance of family from a Christian and common-sense perspective, addressing some of the problems and challenges families face.

Smalley, Gary. *Making Love Last Forever*. Dallas, Tex.: Word, 1996. Understandable and powerful exercises for creating a relationship that is designed to last forever.

Waite, Linda J. and Maggie Gallagher. *The Case for Marriage: Why Married People Are Happier, Healthier, and Better Off Financially*. New York: Doubleday, 2000. Debunks the myths of the "postmarriage culture" and makes a compelling case for the extraordinary benefits of marriage.

Communication and Relationships

Gray, John. *Men Are from Mars, Women Are from Venus*. New York: Harper Collins, 1992. Although written for a secular audience and missing much of the meaning of the covenant of marriage, a few of the works by Dr. John Gray may be helpful in understanding the difference in communication styles between the sexes.

—. *What Your Mother Couldn't Tell You and Your Father Didn't Know: Advanced Relationship Skills for Better Communication and Lasting Intimacy.* New York: Harper Collins, 1994.

Wheat, Ed and Gloria Perkins. *Secret Choices: How to Settle Little Issues before They Become Big Problems.* Grand Rapids, Mich.: Zondervan, 1994. How adults can handle decision making and the potential impact these choices can have on your marriage.

Wright, H. Norman. *Communication: Key to Your Marriage.* Ventura, Calif.: Regal Books, 2000.

Wright, H. Norman and Gary J. Oliver. *How to Change Your Spouse (without Ruining Your Marriage).* Ann Arbor, Mich.: Servant Publications, 1994.

Wright, H. Norman. *How to Talk to Your Mate.* Wheaton, Ill.: Tyndale, 1989.

Engagement

Philips, Bob. *How Can I Be Sure: Questions to Ask before You Get Married.* Eugene, Ore.: Harvest House, 2000.

Rainey, Dennis. *Preparing for Marriage.* Ventura, Calif.: Gospel Light, 1997.

Rainey, Dennis and Barbara. *Starting Your Marriage Right: What You Need to Know and Do in the Early Years to Make It Last a Lifetime.* Nashville, Tenn.: Thomas Nelson/Word, 2000.

Wright, H. Norman and Wes Roberts. *Before You Say "I Do."* Eugene, Ore.: Harvest House, 1997.

Wright, H. Norman. *So You're Getting Married: The Keys to Building a Strong and Lasting Relationship.* Ventura, Calif.: Regal Books, 1985.

Finances

Blue, Ron. *Master Your Money*. Nashville, Tenn.: Thomas Nelson, 1997.

—-. *Mastering Money in Your Marriage*. Loveland, Colo.: Group Publishing, 2000.

—-. *Taming the Money Monster: 5 Steps to Conquering Debt*. Colorado Springs: Focus on the Family Publishing, 2000.

Blue, Ron and Judy. *Raising Money-Smart Kids: How to Teach Your Children the Secrets of Earning, Saving, Investing, and Spending Wisely*. Nashville, Tenn.: Thomas Nelson, 1992.

Burkett, Larry. *Debt-Free Living: How to Get Out of Debt and Stay Out*. Chicago: Moody, 2000.

—-. *Generous Living: Discovering the Freedom of Generous Living*. Grand Rapids, Mich.: Zondervan, 1997.

—-. *Giving & Tithing Includes Serving and Stewardship*. Chicago: Moody, 1998.

—-. *How to Manage Your Money*. Chicago: Moody, 2000.

—-. *Money before Marriage: A Financial Workbook for Engaged Couples*. Chicago: Moody, 1996.

—-.*The Family Financial Workbook: A Practical Guide to Budgeting*. Chicago: Moody, 2000.

Kay, Ellie. *How to Save Money Every Day*. Bloomington, Minn.: Bethany House, 2001.

Parrott, Les and Leslie. *Saving Your Marriage before It Starts: Seven Questions to Ask before (and after) You Marry*. Grand Rapids, Mich.: Zondervan, 1995.

Love and Sex

Balswick, Judith and Jack. *Authentic Human Sexuality*. Downers Grove, Ill.: InterVarsity Press, 1999.

Dillow, Linda and Lorraine Pintus. *Intimate Issues: 21*

Questions Christian Women Ask about Sex. Colorado Springs: Waterbrook, 1999.

Gray, John. *Mars and Venus in the Bedroom: A Guide to Lasting Romance and Passion*. New York: Harper Collins, 1996. See previous note about his works.

LaHaye, Tim and Beverly. *The Act of Marriage: The Beauty of Married Life*. Grand Rapids, Mich.: Zondervan, 1976. One of the classics for building a Christian relationship.

Leman, Dr. Kevin. *Sex Begins in the Kitchen: Because Love Is an All-Day Affair*. Grand Rapids, Mich.: Baker/Revell, 1999.

Penner, Clifford. *The Gift of Sex: A Guide to Sexual Fulfillment*. Dallas, Tex.: Word, 1981.

Penner, Clifford and Joyce. *Getting Your Sex Life Off to a Great Start*. Dallas, Tex.: Word, 1994.

—. *Restoring the Pleasure*. Dallas, Tex.: Word, 1993.

—. *What Every Wife Wants Her Husband to Know about Sex*. Nashville, Tenn.: Thomas Nelson, 1998.

Rainey, Dennis. *Lonely Husbands, Lonely Wives: Rekindling Intimacy in Every Marriage*. Dallas, Tex.: Word, 1989.

Rainey, Dennis and Barbara. *Simply Romantic Nights*. Little Rock, Ark.: FamilyLife, 2001.

Rosenau, Dr. Douglas. *A Celebration of Sex*. Nashville, Tenn.: Thomas Nelson/Word, 1994.

Wheat, Ed and Gaye, *Intended for Pleasure*. Grand Rapids, Mich.: Baker, 1981.

Wheat, Ed and Gloria Perkins, *Love Life for Every Married Couple*. Grand Rapids, Mich.: Zondervan, 1980.

Prayer

Dobson, James and Shirley. *Night Light: A Devotional for Couples*. Sisters, Ore.: Multnomah, 2000.

Rainey, Dennis and Barbara. *Moments Together for Couples*. Ventura, Calif.: Regal Books, 1995.

Wright, H. Norman. *Starting Out Together Couples Devotional*. Ventura, Calif.: Regal Books, 1996.

—. *Quiet Times for Couples*. Eugene, Ore.: Harvest House, 2000.

Web sites

The following represent a sampling of Internet resources available on some of the subjects addressed in this book. There are literally thousands of good sites on these subjects, and many provide articles, suggestions, links, and stories that might be helpful to you in building your marriage. A word of caution: There are many, many Web sites out there that purport to be marriage- or family-oriented. Unfortunately, some of these sites are only opportunities for those selling a service or product or advocates of some narrow agenda. Use the Web with caution and discretion, and focus on sites that are managed by ministries or organizations with which you are familiar.

FOCUS ON THE FAMILY: WWW.FAMILY.ORG

The ministry founded by Dr. James Dobson has many resources related to relationships, marriage, children, and faith. Dobson's *Dare to Discipline* was the single most influential book in our own education about child-rearing.

Focus provides an extensive listing of premarital and marital resources. The books, articles, devotionals, and seminars are an excellent foundation for any couple. Focus maintains a separate Web site for marriage at www.family.org/married. Topics include women, engagement, newlyweds, sex & romance, communication, and finances.

HERITAGE FOUNDATION: WWW.HERITAGE.ORG
Heritage policy experts provide background, speeches, and data analysis on marriage and its impact on society.

MARRIAGE SAVERS: WWW.MARRIAGESAVERS.ORG
Marriage Savers, founded by Mike and Harriet McManus, has helped churches and metropolitan areas strengthen marriages and push down divorce rates.

STRONG MARRIAGES: WWW.STRONGMARRIAGES.ORG
A ministry with several marriage support services.

THE FATHERHOOD INITIATIVE: WWW.FATHERHOOD.ORG
The mission of the National Fatherhood Initiative (NFI) is to stimulate a society-wide movement to confront the growing problem of father absence and is dedicated to improving the well-being of children by increasing the number of children growing up with involved, committed, and responsible fathers in their lives.

CONCERNED WOMEN FOR AMERICA: WWW.CWFA.ORG
Concerned Women for America, with members in fifty states, is the largest public policy women's organization in the nation. Although CWA is primarily a women's organization, deals with the family, so men are also encouraged to join. Its membership includes women and men of all ages, church affiliations, and political parties.

MARRIAGE SUPPORT: WWW.COUPLES-PLACE.COM
A secular on-line learning community for "solving marriage problems, improving relationship skills, celebrating marriage, and achieving happiness with your partner."

COVENANT MARRIAGE: WWW.DIVORCEREFORM.ORG
Sponsored by Americans for Divorce Reform, this site lists all of the relevant links for covenant marriage information.

FAMILY LIFE: WWW.FAMILYLIFE.COM
A division of Campus Crusade for Christ that is dedicated to building strong families. They sponsor marriage aids such as the Home Builders series, couples devotionals, and Dennis Rainey's commentaries.

MARRIAGE BUILDERS: WWW.MARRIAGEBUILDERS.COM
A secular site, but one with lots of links to marriage support services.

Notes

Introduction

1. Barna Research Online, "Christians are More Likely to Experience Divorce than Are Non-Christians," www.barna.org, December 21, 1999. Barna is a well-established research and polling organization that tracks issues of interest to Christians. As with any study, it is important to look not only at the methodology, but also at the questions asked and the respondent pool. The study further broke down the divorce rate among Christian denominations and a number of other religions, which shows that no faith tradition can make marriage guarantees. The numbers for Christian denominations were as follows: Baptists—29 percent have divorced; Catholics—21 percent; Nondenominational Protestant—34 percent; Lutherans—21 percent; mainline Protestant churches—25 percent. A surprise to me: The divorce rate among Protestant senior pastors is 15 percent.

2. David Popenoe and Barbara Dafoe Whitehead, "The State of Our Unions 2000," *The National Marriage Project 2000* (Rutgers University). One commentator, William Mattox, has warned about the danger of using these statistics.

Rather than demoralize or frighten newly married couples, we need to encourage the sense that they do not need to live out these trends and can counter them by taking marriage seriously, a sentiment I strongly support.

Chapter 2: Forming Families

1. "The Celebration and Blessing of a Marriage," *The Book of Common Prayer* (New York: The Church Hymnal Corporation, 1979), 423.
2. William R. Mattox Jr., "Aha! Call It the Revenge of the Church Ladies," *USA Today*, 11 February 1999.
3. John Paul II, Encyclical Letter *Centesimus Annus* (1 May 1991), 39.
4. Edith Schaeffer, *What Is a Family?* (Grand Rapids, Mich.: Baker Book House, 1975), 81.

Chapter 3: Understanding *Forever*

1. The Council on Families in America, *Marriage in America: A Report to the Nation* (New York: Institute for American Values), 4 April 1995.
2. In 1940, there were 264,000 divorces and annulments, a rate of two per one thousand women. The Centers for Disease Control and Prevention, "Divorce and Annulments and Rates: United States, 1940–90," (National Center for Health Statistics) *Monthly Vital Statistics Report* 43, no. 9 (March 1995).
3. The Centers for Disease Control and Prevention, "Births, Marriages, Divorces, and Death: Provisional Data for 1998," (National Center for Health Statistics) *National Vital Statistics Report* 47, no. 21 (July 1999).

4. Nancy Reagan, *I Love You, Ronnie: The Letters of Ronald Reagan to Nancy Reagan* (New York: Random House, 2000), 78.

Chapter 4: The Choice for Children

1. Patrick Fagan, "How Broken Families Rob Their Children of Their Chances for Future Prosperity," *Heritage Foundation Backgrounder*, 11 June 1999. In addition, divorce is often the cause of this poverty. "Almost half of American families experience poverty following a divorce, and 75 percent of all women who apply for welfare benefits do so because of a disrupted marriage or disputed relationship."
2. Edith Schaeffer, *What Is a Family?* (Grand Rapids, Mich.: Baker Books, 1975), 62.
3. Robert Fulghum, *It Was on Fire When I Lay down on It* (New York: Villard Books, 1989), 103.

Chapter 5: "Work" Versus "Career"

1. Edith Schaeffer, *A Celebration of Marriage* (Grand Rapids, Mich.: Baker Books, 1994), 44.

Chapter 6: Preventative Care

1. Scott M. Stanley, "Decoding Census Data," University of Denver Center for Marital and Family Studies, found at *www.smartmarriages.com/divorcestats.html*.

Chapter 7: Uncrossing Communications

1. Logan Pearsall Smith, *Afterthoughts* (London: Constable & Co., 1931), 1.

Chapter 9: Intimacy Versus Sex

1. Edward Laumann, et al., "Sexual Dysfunction in the United States: Prevalence and Predictors," *Journal of the American Medical Association,* 10 February 1999.
2. Ibid.

Chapter 10: Coping with Abuse

1. Bureau of Justice Statistics, "Intimate Partner Violence," U.S. Department of Justice, Office of Justice Programs, May 2000.

Chapter 11: Crisis Points

1. *American Heritage Dictionary of the English Language,* 1996, s.v. "crisis."